THE DAILY SHOW WITH TREVOR NOAH PRESENTS

THE

DONALD J. TRUMP

★ PRESIDENTIAL TWITTER LIBRARY ★

THE DAILY SHOW WITH TREVOR NOAH PRESENTS

THE

DONALD J. TRUMP

★ PRESIDENTIAL TWITTER LIBRARY ★

COMEDY CENTRAL

SPIEGEL & GRAU

New York

THE DAILY SHOW WITH TREVOR NOAH PRESENTS

THE

DONALD J. TRUMP

★ PRESIDENTIAL TWITTER LIBRARY ★

EDITOR • Steve Bodow

MANAGING EDITOR • Jen Flanz

CHIEF CURATOR • Ramin Hedayati   **HEAD WRITERS** • Steve Bodow, Daniel Radosh

WRITERS • Amberia Allen, Dan Amira, David Angelo, Devin Delliquanti, Zach DiLanzo, Geoff Haggerty, Ramin Hedayati, Josh Johnson, Matt Koff, Dan McCoy, Lauren Sarver Means, Matt Negrin, Joseph Opio, Zhubin Parang, Kat Radley, Scott Sherman, Colleen Werthmann

PRODUCED BY • Jocelyn Conn

CONTENT PRODUCERS • Matt Negrin, Ant DeRosa

ART DIRECTION AND DESIGN • Angelina Battista, Paulina Niewinska, Erin Smith, and Simon Sullivan

DESIGN/PRODUCTION SUPERVISOR (COMEDY CENTRAL) • Donna Tine

ART • Joe Dettmore, Katie Hall, Dave Heiss, Michael Hogan

ELEMENT PRODUCERS • Elise Terrell, Shawna Shepherd, Beth Shorr, Dave Blog, Adam Chodikoff, Nick Dyer

EDITORIAL ASSISTANT • Katie Maraghy

**GEORGE
WASHINGTON**
1789 – 1797

**ABRAHAM
LINCOLN**
1861 – 1865

**FRANKLIN
DELANO
ROOSEVELT**
1933 – 1945

"Many people have said
I'm the world's greatest writer of
140 character sentences."

DONALD J. TRUMP, TWITTER
4:50 PM - 21 Jul 2014

JOHN F.
KENNEDY
1961 – 1963

BILL
CLINTON
1993 – 2001

DONALD J.
TRUMP
2017 – TBD

TABLE

OF

CONTENTS

———————

★

PLEASE ENJOY IN MODERATION, IF THERE'S EVEN SUCH A THING ANYMORE.

INTRODUCTION

When Donald J. Trump launched his campaign for president in 2015, I laughed at the idea. If there's one thing I knew about Americans, it's that they wanted their presidents to be dignified, intelligent, and black. Trump had none of these qualities. Even worse, Trump had tweets!

Years and years of tweets, thousands of them, on everything from why Diet Coke doesn't work to the fact that he is "just not a fan of sharks." Who would vote to give the nuclear codes to a man who had tweet-demanded that Robert Pattinson dump Kristen Stewart?

But as Trump's campaign grew into the movement that would sweep him into the White House, I realized that the opposite was true. Trump's Twitter account didn't disqualify him. It humanized him. Here was a man who didn't filter his statements through focus groups or polling consultants—he said what we were all thinking. Or, at least, what he was all thinking. Like how "The worst show in Las Vegas, in my opinion, is @pennjillette. Hokey garbage. New York show even worse!" It's what Americans needed to hear, and Donald Trump was the only presidential candidate saying it.

We at *The Daily Show* realized that we must honor this archive of presidential thoughts. Thus was born *The Donald J. Trump Presidential Twitter Library*, a curated collection of Trump's most profound and revealing tweets that allowed everyday Americans to literally walk through the President's mind. After successful openings in New York, Chicago, San Francisco, and Los Angeles, the Library now takes form in this keepsake book, so that you, dear reader, can cherish the experience in the comfort of home.

Please read these tweets in the spirit in which they were composed: with an open heart and with legs straddling the toilet of your choice.

TREVOR NOAH

FOREWORD

Late on the afternoon of Monday, June 30, 1941, Franklin D. Roosevelt spoke at the dedication of his newly constructed presidential library at Hyde Park, New York, the first of its kind in American history. "To bring together the records of the past . . . where they will be preserved for the use of men and women in the future, a Nation must believe in three things," President Roosevelt told the crowd. "It must believe in the past. It must believe in the future. It must, above all, believe in the capacity of its own people so to learn from the past that they can gain in judgment in creating their own future."

It wasn't exactly a Twitter-friendly message. But FDR's point, if verbose, was simple: Thanks to his efforts then, our generation today would be wiser than the one that elected him. And who's to say he was wrong?

Given the 2016 presidential election and its aftermath, I am. As a presidential historian, I might have been asked to pen an introduction to the libraries of Roosevelt or Kennedy or one of the Bushes. But instead, my assignment, which I for some reason accepted, is to write 750 words on The Donald J. Trump Presidential Twitter Library. The J. stands for John, and per my lawyer counts as a word.

So Trump may not be FDR, but that is not to say his ever-growing collection of tweets is without historical value. On the contrary. Commanders-in-chief have always been early adopters of the latest means of communication. Lincoln installed a telegraph in the War Department. In 1877, the first White House telephone line enchanted Rutherford Hayes. Calvin Coolidge, notoriously a man of few words, used up a handful of them to reach 23 million radio listeners in his 1925 inaugural, and of course Roosevelt's fireside chats ushered in the now familiar practice of staring dead-eyed at an electronic media device and hoping to feel something, anything. Truman became the first president to deliver a televised address in 1947. Bill Clinton brought the Oval Office into the Digital Age, sending the first presidential email, though it was later mysteriously deleted by an unknown party in his household.

And now the digital ruminations of the 45th president give us that rarest thing: a running record of a president's moods and musings. While Woodrow Wilson once observed that a presidency offers its occupant the opportunity to be as big a man as he wants to be, the Trump canon is a chronicle of just how small a president can be. Trump is not the first president to obsess over his opponents and to rant about the seeming injustice of the world. He's just the first to make the rest of us listen in as he does it.

With that in mind, the closest parallel to President Trump's tweets should give him no comfort, for the precedent is not FDR's millions of cubic feet of records or Lincoln's reams of manuscripts or Jefferson's thousands of letters. It is the covert White House recordings of Richard M. Nixon, who destroyed his own presidency by allowing his darkest machinations to be captured on audiotape.

Trump partisans, of course, demur, arguing that he (or as he might put it, he "alone") understands how Twitter eliminates the filter of a hostile press, giving the people what they want: All Trump, All the Time.

Perhaps, but that brings us back to FDR, who felt otherwise. "The public psychology and, for that matter, individual psychology cannot, because of human weakness, be attuned for long periods of time to a constant repetition of the highest note in the scale," Roosevelt wrote in a 1935 letter. "People tire of seeing the same name day after day in the important headlines of the papers, and the same voice night after night over the radio." A leader's balancing act, then, was the education and shaping of public opinion without becoming overly familiar or exhausting.

Trump believes the opposite. For him, attention is all. As president, he has raised narcissism to Homeric heights— a difficult thing to do when one recalls that politicians, as a species, consider public notice to be slightly more essential than oxygen. But here we are. He's not going to stop.

And so our evaluation of the historical significance of Trump's tweets brings us to this frightful but urgent conclusion: With the very future of the Republic hanging in the balance, it is imperative that 746, 747, 748, the end.

JON MEACHAM

THE DONALD J. TRUMP PRESIDENTIAL TWITTER LIBRARY

Presidential libraries have long been a cherished destination for school trips when the amusement park is too expensive. *The Daily Show Presents: The Donald J. Trump Presidential Twitter Library* continues this grand tradition with a celebration of President Trump's most important documents: his tweets.

An entire library devoted to one person's tweets may seem "excessive," "unwarranted," or "pretty clearly some kind of publicity stunt." But the way a president chooses to communicate with the public is often what will define his (the "his" streak lives!) legacy. Indeed, when an average American is asked, "What comes to mind when you think of Donald Trump?" the response is likely to be a short burst of pure, unfiltered, inchoate emotion—in other words, something quite similar to a Trump tweet. That's how much Trump's Twitter output has come to shape not only his presidency but the entire era we are now all so fortunate to be surviving.

But becoming the communications genius he is today took a lifetime of being the communications genius he was before today.

BEGINNINGS

Attempts to reconstruct the pre-Twitter life of Donald J. Trump are unavoidably incomplete, as he was not yet finger-banging out his every unedited thought. We do know that Trump was born in Queens, New York, on Flag Day 1946, nine months after the first and, at press time, last wartime use of nuclear weapons. After a hugely successful toddlerhood, young Donald moved on to the best schools, where he showed great promise as a negotiator, claiming, for example, to have once settled a dispute with a music teacher by punching him in the face. High school was at New York Military Academy, where Trump gained the training he would need in Vietnam, if he ever went to Vietnam, which he didn't. Instead Trump studied business at Wharton. That's one of the top places in the country, where only really smart people go.

Then the young man cast out on his own, at first subsisting on only a tiny million-dollar

loan from his father. Donald soon launched a career in real estate, becoming the first Trump to do so in almost one generation. It was the 1970s. Few saw value in Manhattan, which at the time was less a city and more a floating porn-and-murder barge. But something about a morally bankrupt, money-obsessed smut-scape spoke to Donald Trump. By the time he was 35, Trump had begun to make a name for himself, plant that name in tabloid gossip columns, and then license that name to people who actually made buildings.

After defeating New York, it was on to Atlantic City, where Trump mastered the local hotel-casino game. Yes, at one point Trump's casinos did hit a bit of a multi-billion-dollar financial rough spot. Yet using only gumption and lawyers, Trump quickly rose all the way from bankruptcy, to another bankruptcy, to two more bankruptcies.

The new millennium found Trump making his first presidential run on a platform promising universal healthcare, cutting the federal deficit, and marrying his supermodel girlfriend. But like a stripper at a bar mitzvah, it was too soon.

Happily, in 2004, Donald discovered the business he was truly meant for: fake business. *The Apprentice* went on to become, by at least one man's account, the most popular series in the history of television.

Donald Trump seemed to have it all. Money. Fame. And no beliefs to slow him down. But he wouldn't be satisfied until he could share his wisdom directly with the American people.

TWITTER

On May 4, 2009, a visionary billionaire logged on to an upstart messaging website, put thumbs to screen, typed a promotional message for his upcoming appearance on David Letterman, and hit send.

Donald J. Trump @realDonaldTrump Following

Be sure to tune in and watch Donald Trump on Late Night with David Letterman as he presents the Top Ten List tonight!

11:54 AM - 4 May 2009

It was Donald J. Trump's first tweet. And though he used the name of the wrong Letterman show, it was a moment that would change America forever.

Trump warmed quickly to his new account, which he named "@realDonaldTrump" to prevent imposters from posting tweets that might be embarrassing. Twitter was the ideal medium for the future president: fast, no limits, grammar super-optional. With tweets, he could finally express who the @realDonaldTrump was. The world would now know: These were the things this actual

person actually believed were worth writing in public.

Donald J. Trump @realDonaldTrump Following

The Mar-a-Lago Club has the best meatloaf in America. Tasty.
maralagoclub.com/

10:23 AM - 29 Dec 2011

In the ensuing years and tens of thousands of tweets, Trump cultivated a rhetorical style that projected strength strongly, through brute aggression towards everything from celebrities to TV shows to apex predators.

Donald J. Trump @realDonaldTrump Following

Sharks are last on my list - other than perhaps the losers and haters of the World!

7:28 AM - 4 Jul 2013

As one can imagine, speaking such truth to power quickly earned Trump many enemies. But the POTUS-in-waiting refused to be silenced by fear or taste. He launched regular tirades against any perceived foe, offering olive branches only on America's most sacred of days.

Donald J. Trump @realDonaldTrump Following

"@realDonaldTrump: I would like to extend my best wishes to all, even the haters and losers, on this special date, September 11th."

8:12 PM - 11 Sep 2013

Besides, @realDonaldTrump was far more than just a professional grudge generator. The account often let a fascinated public glimpse into the president-to-be's private life. We saw, for example, Donald play the

part of doting husband with future FLOTUS Melania.

Donald J. Trump @realDonaldTrump Following

Turn to QVC now to watch Melania - really good stuff!

5:20 PM - 2 May 2013

Trump's love for his most recent wife sparkled as bright as the high-quality gems she sold on television at such fantastic prices.

Yet with the advantage of some historical distance, we see now that first and foremost, @realDonaldTrump marks Trump irreducibly as a man of his time. For as America's political climate darkened during the Obama presidency, Donald Trump seemed instinctively to set aside his celebrity feuds and fringe conspiracies for serious political discourse.

THE CANDIDATE

Thanks to his tweets, Donald Trump soon established himself as a leader of the "birther" movement, which only grew stronger as President Obama failed time and again to prove that he was white

enough to have been born in the United States.

Trump's leadership on the issue was well-timed. By 2015, conservative voters were furious at Obama and looking for a presidential candidate with the most anti-Obama credentials, no matter how ludicrous. This was Donald Trump's moment. In June 2015, he declared he was running for president.

Trump's candidacy flourished, in no small part thanks to his tweets. Even as his time became more in demand, Donald Trump was digitally relentless, often retweeting those whom society had marginalized, such as white supremacists, neo-Nazis, and other very fine people on both sides.

Trump's appeal to the Forgotten Nazi worked. By early 2016, he had vanquished seventeen Lyin', Low Energy, and Truly Weird competitors on his way to securing the Republican nomination.

Donald J. Trump
@realDonaldTrump

Following

Truly weird Senator Rand Paul of Kentucky reminds me of a spoiled brat without a properly functioning brain. He was terrible at DEBATE!

8:41 PM - 10 Aug 2015

His evolution from pop-culture polemicist to populist political firebrand was complete.

THE 2016 ELECTION (WON BY TRUMP)

November 8, 2016: a day none of us shall soon forget. Twitter helped Trump cruise to an easy victory over Crooked Hillary Clinton, defeating her in the electoral college and the popular vote, once the millions of illegal votes were deducted.

@REALPRESIDENT OFTHEUNITEDSTATES

Some questioned whether Trump would continue tweeting postinauguration— once he had assumed the full mantle of responsibilities that come with the world's most important job. Remember, too, that at that long-ago time, terse, idiosyncratically punctuated online diatribes were not yet considered "presidential."

Even the president-elect himself felt conflicted, lamenting the very need for tweets:

Donald J. Trump
@realDonaldTrump

Following

If the press would cover me accurately & honorably, I would have far less reason to "tweet." Sadly, I don't know if that will ever happen!

8:00 AM - 5 Dec 2016

Yet once in office, the seventy-year-old Trump would keep tweeting with the vigor of a person sixty years his junior.

THE TRUMP LEGACY

At this writing, midway through his first term, President Donald Trump relies more than ever on Twitter, now his chief tool for demolishing roadblocks, such as the legislature and the press. As the former surrenders to his executive authority and the latter vanishes into the mysteries of social media algorithms, now is as good a time, and possibly nearing the end of time, to publish a book on the tweets that made it all happen.

The Daily Show Presents: The Donald J. Trump Presidential Twitter Library curates a comprehensive selection of tweets, retweets, @-replies, and images pulled from Donald J. Trump's prolific twitterary output of more than 37,000 pieces, exploring the history, art, and science of the 45th president's tweets—from his earliest attempts to put totally normal fingers to phone, to his emergence as our era's preeminent social media revolutionary.

As a matter of historical record, we present all Trump tweets "as tweeted." None have been edited in any way, nor have we corrected spelling or grammar in the many instances where they failed to match our subject's "alternative" standards. What emerges, we believe, is an indelible (not to say "unimpeachable") portrait of America's 45th commander-in-chief—and also, for better or worse, of the society that elected him, in what was one of the biggest electoral college wins of all time. Everyone says so.

MP
CAKE

★ ★ ★

#TRUMPCAKE

TERRIFIC HISTORY
THE TRUMP TWITTER TIMELINE

★ BEFORE TWITTER ★
1946–2008: 0 TWEETS

Emerging from the primordial pre-Twitter ooze, Donald J. Trump, an aspiring real estate developer and minor tabloid celebrity, anticipates the coming medium with his own unique form of communication: commenting on things he doesn't like by scrawling his remarks in Sharpie and mailing them to people.

★ THE BRONZER AGE ★

2009: 56 TWEETS   2010: 155 TWEETS

Trump displays an early fascination with building walls

 "My persona will never be that of a wallflower - I'd rather build walls than cling to them" -- Donald J. Trump

12 May 2009

Proof that Donald Trump once spent time with his wife

 Melania and I saw American Idiot on Broadway last night and it was great. An amazing theatrical experience!

21 April 2010

Trump congratulates his main daughter on her marriage to the real estate heir who will one day be tasked with brokering Mideast peace

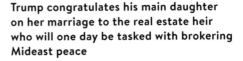 -- From Donald Trump: "Ivanka and Jared's wedding was spectacular, and they make a beautiful couple. I'm a very proud father."

27 Oct 2009

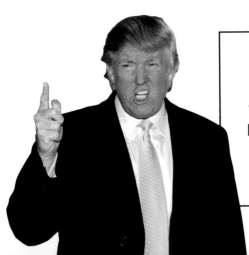

★

Trump's historic first tweet, likely written by his caddy/social media coordinator

"Be sure to tune in and watch Donald Trump on Late Night with David Letterman as he presents the Top Ten List tonight!"

4 May 2009

The future 45th president stars in a groundbreaking Serta mattress web series

 Check out the last webisode in our 3 part series featuring me with Serta. Which one was your favorite?

12 Aug 2010

Trump decides not to run for president, disappointed nation begins a four-year wait

 This has been a very difficult decision regarding the Presidential run and I want to thank all my twitter fans for your fantastic support.

16 May 2011

Trump discovers a groundbreaking new form of therapy: cyberbullying. Confirms that he has yet to obtain professional psychiatric help.

 It makes me feel so good to hit "sleazebags" back -- much better than seeing a psychiatrist (which I never have!)

19 Nov 2012

Trump first devises ingenious shorthand for the many haters and losers in his life: "haters and losers"

 It's okay but why do the haters (& losers) want to follow me on twitter?? Get a life!

12 Feb 2013

> "Be prepared, there is a small chance that our
> horrendous leadership could unknowingly lead us into World War III."
> 31 Aug 2013

★ THE CRANIUM EXPLOSION ★

2011: 963 TWEETS   **2012: 4585 TWEETS**   **2013: 8731 TWEETS**

Trump begins friendship with Pulitzer-aware opinion journalist Sean Hannity

 Watched Sean Hannity last night -- a great guy.

29 Jul 2011

First attack on classless loser Rosie O'Donnell

Please send a psychiatrist to help @Rosie, she's in a bad state. To @Rosie's girlfriend's parents--- get your daughter out of there before it's too late.

15 Dec 2011

The birth of mainstream birtherism

 An 'extremely credible source' has called my office and told me that @BarackObama's birth certificate is a fraud.

6 Aug 2012

First appearance of iconic catchphrase "Sad!"

 Our leaders are terrible. The government spends over $50B a day. It can't find cuts for less than 2 days of spending?! Sad!

25 Feb 2013

Spelling aside, he wasn't wrong

@MileyCyrus is on a very triky and slippery path right now. The right moves will lead to greatness, the wrong moves to oblivion! GUIDANCE.

8 Oct 2013

Trump warns nation, wishes it luck

 It's almost like the United States has no President - we are a rudderless ship heading for a major disaster. Good luck everyone!

19 Mar 2014

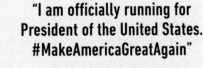

"I am officially running for President of the United States. #MakeAmericaGreatAgain"

16 June 2015

Some Mexicans relieved to hear they might be good people

 Today I officially declared my candidacy for President of the United States. Watch the video of my full speech-

16 Jun 2015

Nevertheless, he persisted

 I am having a really hard time watching @FoxNews.

21 Sep 2015

TV star leads brave fight against "on-the-air" pollution

 Who is paying for that tedious Smokey Bear commercial that is on all the time—enough already!

8 Jan 2015

★ THE FEUDAL PERIOD ★

2014: 7029 TWEETS   **2015: 9182 TWEETS**

A future leader reflects on his predecessor's legacy

 Sadly, because president Obama has done such a poor job as president, you won't see another black president for generations!

25 Nov 2014

First mention of "failing New York Times"

 Dummy Bill Maher did an advertisement for the failing New York Times where the picture of him is very sad-he looks pathetic, bloated & gone!

23 Dec 2014

Trump crafts sensitive response to the Charlie Hebdo killings in Paris

 If the morons who killed all of those people at Charlie Hebdo would have just waited, the magazine would have folded - no money, no success!

14 Jan 2015

Funk-pop aficionado DJT beta-tests famed "more lawyers" defense strategy

 Boy did Pharrell & Robin Thicke get screwed. The Marvin Gaye song sounds nothing like theirs. Get new lawyers fast!

13 Mar 2015

Trump gets it: everyone loves comedy about his tweets

 I am at the Saturday Night Live Studio - electricity all over the place. We will be doing a "tweeting" skit, so stay tuned!

7 Nov 2015

Going above and beyond as usual, Trump not only orders a medical report, but also writes it himself

 As a presidential candidate, I have instructed my long-time doctor to issue, within two weeks, a full medical report-it will show perfection

3 Dec 2015

Trump wins election, immediately begins implementing hat-based agenda

"TODAY WE MAKE AMERICA GREAT AGAIN!"

8 Nov 2016

Candidate Trump bestows upon Hillary her formal nickname, coronating her as his forever-nemesis

 Crooked Hillary Clinton is spending a fortune on ads against me. I am the one person she doesn't want to run against. Will be such fun!

17 Apr 2016

Six months into 2017, Trump's 2016 campaign reaches a fever pitch

 Crooked H destroyed phones w/ hammer, 'bleached' emails, & had husband meet w/AG days before she was cleared– & they talk about obstruction?

15 Jun 2017

Donald Trump: Master of Interrogation

 I strongly pressed President Putin twice about Russian meddling in our election. He vehemently denied it. I've already given my opinion.....

9 Jul 2017

Definitely not a vacation

 Working in Bedminster, N.J., as long planned construction is being done at the White House. This is not a vacation - meetings and calls!

5 Aug 2017

President Trump launches a devastating nukename at Kim Jong-un

 Just heard Foreign Minister of North Korea speak at U.N. If he echoes thoughts of Little Rocket Man, they won't be around much longer!

23 Sept 2017

★ THE CAMPAIGN PHASE ★

2016: 5342 TWEETS

Campaigning on the issues

 Did Crooked Hillary help disgusting (check out sex tape and past) Alicia M become a U.S. citizen so she could use her in the debate?

30 Sept 2016

Trump explains why sexual assault actually not that big a deal when you think about it

 I'm not proud of my lockerroom talk. But this world has serious problems. We need serious leaders. #debate #BigLeagueTruth

9 Oct 2016

The president-elect demands recount of election he won

 In addition to winning the Electoral College in a landslide, I won the popular vote if you deduct the millions of people who voted illegally

27 Nov 2016

POTUS thanks advisers for his daily intelligence briefing

 Great reporting by @foxandfriends and so many others. Thank you!

9 Jul 2017

First instance of a president making military policy on Twitter, replacing traditional method of "contacting the Department of Defense"

 After consultation with my Generals and military experts, please be advised that the United States Government will not accept or allow......
....Transgender individuals to serve in any capacity in the U.S. Military. Our military must be focused on decisive and overwhelming.....
....victory and cannot be burdened with the tremendous medical costs and disruption that transgender in the military would entail. Thank you

26 Jul 2017

Having fixed all of the problems plaguing the federal government, President Trump sets his sights on professional sports

 The NFL has all sorts of rules and regulations. The only way out for them is to set a rule that you can't kneel during our National Anthem!

26 Sept 2017

Sadly, few Puerto Ricans saw these tweets, because their electrical grid was being lazy

 ...Such poor leadership ability by the Mayor of San Juan, and others in Puerto Rico, who are not able to get their workers to help. They....

...want everything to be done for them when it should be a community effort. 10,000 Federal workers now on Island doing a fantastic job.

30 Sep 2017

Trump makes clear: Under him, the U.S. will NEVER negotiate with journalists

 Time Magazine called to say that I was PROBABLY going to be named "Man (Person) of the Year," like last year, but I would have to agree to an interview and a major photo shoot. I said probably is no good and took a pass. Thanks anyway!

24 Nov 2017

Trump's "most-watched SotU in history" all the more impressive for having been watched by fewer people than SotU's by Obama, Clinton, and Bush

 Thank you for all of the nice compliments and reviews on the State of the Union speech. 45.6 million people watched, the highest number in history. @FoxNews beat every other Network, for the first time ever, with 11.7 million people tuning in. Delivered from the heart!

1 Feb 2018

Praising the NRA one day after publicly advocating strict new gun laws highlights POTUS's ability to listen to, strongly agree with, and also do nothing about both sides of an argument

 Good (Great) meeting in the Oval Office tonight with the NRA!

1 Mar 2018

Stable genius recognize stable genius

 Thank you Kanye, very cool!

25 Apr 2018

KANYE WEST @Kanyewest
You don't have to agree with trump but the mob can't make me not love him. We are both dragon energy. He is my brother. I love everyone. I don't agree with everything anyone does. That's what makes us individuals. And we have the right to independent thought.

★ COMMANDER-IN-TWEET ★

2017: 2594 TWEETS   2018: 2413 TWEETS (PROJECTED)

Trump dislikes social media, according to his 22nd tweet of the week

 I use Social Media not because I like to, but because it is the only way to fight a VERY dishonest and unfair "press," now often referred to as Fake News Media. Phony and non-existent "sources" are being used more often than ever. Many stories & reports a pure fiction!

30 Dec 2017

President issues harshest indictment of Jay-Z since *Lemonade*

 Somebody please inform Jay-Z that because of my policies, Black Unemployment has just been reported to be at the LOWEST RATE EVER RECORDED!

28 Jan 2018

First use of Twitter to fire a cabinet secretary, which, like losing virginity, is always best done in public

 Mike Pompeo, Director of the CIA, will become our new Secretary of State. He will do a fantastic job! Thank you to Rex Tillerson for his service! Gina Haspel will become the new Director of the CIA, and the first woman so chosen. Congratulations to all!

13 Mar 2018

President celebrates the only fire effectively put out during his administration

 Fire at Trump Tower is out. Very confined (well built building). Firemen (and women) did a great job. THANK YOU!

7 Apr 2018

POTUS's wife was sic, but fortunately got better

 Great to have our incredible First Lady back home in the White House. Melanie is feeling and doing really well. Thank you for all of your prayers and best wishes!

19 May 2018

"My use of social media is not Presidential - it's MODERN DAY PRESIDENTIAL. Make America Great Again!"

1 Jul 2017

★ ★ ★

MASTERWORKS

★ ★ ★

"BIRTH OF A BIRTHER"

6 AUG 2012 - 4:23 PM

MEDIUM: TWITTER WEB CLIENT

DIMENSIONS: 113 CHARACTERS

Critics may disagree on the greatest of Trump's tweets, but all cite "Birth of a Birther" as his first unquestionable masterpiece. Taken as a standalone work, one can marvel at the audacity of his creative imagination—the delicacy of the halo of quotations encircling "extremely credible source." Yet it is as a preface to Trump's most productive creative period that "Birth of a Birther" finds its true strength—achieving a metaphorical "birthing" of the artist's identity by questioning the literal birth of another. Contradictory forces thus become complementary, as Trump is clearly inspired by the harmonious interplay of yin and yang first described in ancient China, a known currency manipulator.

"9/11 HATERS AND LOSERS"

11 SEP 2013 – 8:12 PM

MEDIUM: TWITTER FOR ANDROID

DIMENSIONS: 131 CHARACTERS

Remembrance. Reverence. Defiance. These traits are on full display in this double-edged salutation that both honors and mocks Trump's critics on the twelfth anniversary of America's deadliest terror attack. A product of late Birther Era angst, the original 7:21 A.M. version of this tweet was deleted circa 2015 (Early Campaign Phase); yet this 8:12 P.M. manual self-retweet, which for some reason was not also deleted, allows the work to live on. These faux-naïf modifications only redouble the tweet's meaning: simultaneously an admission of impropriety and a bold provocation towards the very "haters and losers" he addresses. Though he continued to work in the "insult-comic statesman" genre on subsequent holidays, no other tweet matches the discursive complexity of this confrontational tour de force.

"TACO BOWLS"

5 MAY 2016 – 2:57 PM

MEDIUM: TWITTER FOR IPHONE

DIMENSIONS: 88 CHARACTERS, 1024 X 1365 PHOTO

A decidedly American artist, Trump rarely draws from other creative traditions. Yet here we see him showcasing pride in a Mesoamerican heritage that, for the artist's instant and effortless mastery of the form, may as well be his own. At the same time, the taco bowl's oblique symbolism embodies Trump's trademark patriotism: his is a crisp, crunchy nation, deep-fried and welcoming to all fixin's that yearn to dwell therein, provided they rise to his own Towering standards. Guac is extra.

"LYIN' TED"

22 MAR 2016 – 9:53 PM

MEDIUM: TWITTER FOR ANDROID

DIMENSIONS: 137 CHARACTERS

In the "Primary Phase" of his Campaign period (early 2016), Trump began
to incorporate a number of new characters into his artistic narrative: in
this tweet, the tragic clown "Lyin' Ted Cruz." Historians dispute whether
the actual Cruz was friend or rival to Trump during this period, but what
is clear is that he is presented within the diegesis as Trump's most dogged
yet miserable foil, an inverted ego sculpted from living embarrassment.
Here Trump surreally imagines pouring beans over the body of Lyin' Ted's
spouse—a double cuckolding, given Lyin' Ted's known love for beans and
(one also assumes) his wife.

THE SPECIAL RELATIONSHIP
FOX & FRIENDS & FORTY-FIVE

Long before his big, unprecedented electoral college landslide victory, Donald Trump held the blond-lady-sandwich morning news program *Fox & Friends* in high esteem. He was a frequent *Fox & Friends* guest, and no wonder; the show's rigor, objectivity, and fundamental decency exactly matched Trump's own.

Once Mr. Trump became president, what had begun as friendly, pre-breakfast TV banter on racial purity and vaccines' link to autism evolved into his most important daily intelligence briefing. The "Curvy Couch Cabinet" presented its findings with a flair that normal intel reports couldn't match: jaunty music, unquestioning validation, and glimpses of upper thigh when the middle one crossed her legs.

Perhaps *Fox & Friends*'s most potent tool was its lower-screen headline banner. These simple, concise phrases helped the world's most powerful man form his thoughts, often by presenting him with those thoughts already fully cooked and ready-to-tweet.

26 JAN 2017

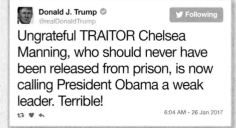

5:50 AM   6:04 AM

18 OCT 2017

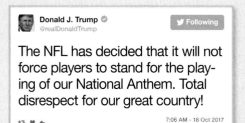

6:27 AM   7:06 AM

19 OCT 2017

6:48 AM   7:56 AM

Donald J. Trump ✓
@realDonaldTrump

🐦 Following

Happy birthday to the great @ TheLeeGreenwood. You and your beautiful song have made such a difference. MAKE AMERICA GREAT AGAIN!

↺ ♥ ↩   7:56 AM - 27 Oct 2017

27 OCT 2017

6:29 AM   7:56 AM

Donald J. Trump ✓
@realDonaldTrump

🐦 Following

Report: "ANTI-TRUMP FBI AGENT LED CLINTON EMAIL PROBE" Now it all starts to make sense!

↺ ♥ ↩   8:36 AM - 3 Dec 2017

3 DEC 2017

8:08 AM   8:36 AM

Donald J. Trump ✓
@realDonaldTrump

🐦 Following

Since taking office I have been very strict on Commercial Aviation. Good news - it was just reported that there were Zero deaths in 2017, the best and safest year on record!

↺ ♥ ↩   9:13 AM - 2 Jan 2018

2 JAN 2018

7:24 AM   9:13 AM

Donald J. Trump ✓
@realDonaldTrump

🐦 Following

Lowest rated Oscars in HISTORY. Problem is, we don't have Stars anymore - except your President (just kidding, of course)!

↺ ♥ ↩   8:25 AM - 6 Mar 2018

6 MAR 2018

7:09 AM   8:25 AM

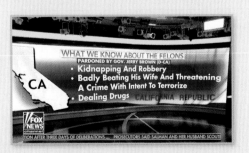

Donald J. Trump ✓
@realDonaldTrump

🐦 Following

Governor Jerry "Moonbeam" Brown pardoned 5 criminal illegal aliens whose crimes include (1) Kidnapping and Robbery (2) Badly beating wife and threatening a crime with intent to terrorize (3) Dealing drugs. Is this really what the great people of California want? @FoxNews

↺ ♥ ↩   8:53 AM - 31 Mar 2018

31 MAR 2018

6:06 AM   8:53 AM

★ ★ ★

GREATEST BATTLES

★ ★ ★

THE SECOND CIVIL WAR

Some presidents believe in reaching across the aisle. Others believe
in taking on the other side. But not until Donald Trump did we have a
president brave enough to mercilessly attack his own party. Trump's
ongoing war against the GOP pits brother against brother, friend
against friend, and everyone against Ted Cruz. It is on this field of
battle that Trump perfected the most devastating weapon in his
Twitter arsenal: the cruel nickname.

★ ★ ★

THE BUSHKRIEG

One of Donald Trump's most decisive victories was over Jeb (Jeb!) Bush. Where some candidates may have seen an unobtrusive family man of basic decency whose poll numbers posed literally zero threat, Trump saw a menace whom he not only had to crush, but to destroy so thoroughly that the shattered fragments of his personality could never be put together again.

★ ★ ★

THE WAR OF
MASCULINE AGGRESSION

No one respects women more than Donald Trump. That's why he has always fought against womankind's intrinsic tendency to make fools and/or sluts of themselves. Boldly challenging insurgent troublemakers like Rosie O'Donnell, Bette Midler, Cher, and victims of sexual assault in the military, Trump emerges from his battles with women proving time and again that his "great respect" will never blind him to their many physical and emotional flaws.

Donald J. Trump @
@realDonaldTrump

.@ariannahuff is unattractive both inside and out. I fully understand why her former husband left her for a man- he made a good decision.

10:54 AM - 28 Aug 2012

Donald J. Trump @
@realDonaldTrump

.@BetteMidler talks about my hair but I'm not allowed to talk about her ugly face or body --- so I won't. Is this a double standard?

11:57 AM - 28 Oct 2012

Donald J. Trump @
@realDonaldTrump

.@cher--I don't wear a "rug"— it's mine. And I promise not to talk about your massive plastic surgeries that didn't work.

3:23 PM - 13 Nov 2012

Donald J. Trump @
@realDonaldTrump

26,000 unreported sexual assults in the military-only 238 convictions. What did these geniuses expect when they put men & women together?

7:04 PM - 7 May 2013

Donald J. Trump @
@realDonaldTrump

Sorry, @Rosie is a mentally sick woman, a bully, a dummy and, above all, a loser. Other than that she is just wonderful!

8:53 PM - 8 Dec 2014

Donald J. Trump @
@realDonaldTrump

I refuse to call Megyn Kelly a bimbo, because that would not be politically correct. Instead I will only call her a lightweight reporter!

6:44 AM - 27 Jan 2016

Donald J. Trump @
@realDonaldTrump

The press is going out of their way to convince people that I do not like or respect women, when they know that it is just the opposite!

3:01 PM - 26 Mar 2016

★ ★ ★

THE BATTLE
OF BULLSHIT RUN

A tragic tale of allies turned against one another, Donald Trump's war with the media could easily have been avoided, if only news outlets had refrained from reporting on things that Trump did or said. He was forced to lay waste to print and television alike, ensuring that no person will ever again hear the word "news" without also thinking "fake."

★ ★ ★

THE DIET COKE REBELLION

Donald Trump's early skirmish with Diet Coke was instrumental in forging his theory of Twitter warfare. Here we track his battle with the "(soda)": from his opening salvo aimed at the drink's lack of appeal to thin people, to his penultimate tweet on the subject, in which Trump bravely admits that his true battle with Diet Coke . . . is in his own heart.

THE NICKNAMES

After his son-in-law Jared, the biggest strategic tool in Donald Trump's rise to national leadership was the disparaging Twitter nickname. Inspired no doubt by the nation's children, Trump devised his now-famous method of placing an insulting descriptor immediately before the name of his antagonist. Below, a selection of the devastating results, along with accompanying first-edition artist's renderings.

CHEATIN' OBAMA

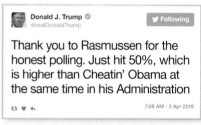

Donald J. Trump
@realDonaldTrump

Thank you to Rasmussen for the honest polling. Just hit 50%, which is higher than Cheatin' Obama at the same time in his Administration

7:08 AM - 3 Apr 2018

CROOKED HILLARY

Donald J. Trump
@realDonaldTrump

Crooked Hillary Clinton blames everybody (and every thing) but herself for her election loss. She lost the debates and lost her direction!

10:47 PM - 13 Sep 2017

LITTLE MARCO

GOOFY ELIZABETH WARREN AKA POCAHONTAS

Donald J. Trump
@realDonaldTrump
Following

Little Marco Rubio, the lightweight no show Senator from Florida, is set to be the "puppet" of the special interest Koch brothers. WATCH!

11:07 AM - 28 Feb 2016

Donald J. Trump
@realDonaldTrump
Following

Goofy Elizabeth Warren, sometimes referred to as Pocahontas, pretended to be a Native American in order to advance her career. Very racist!

7:28 PM - 11 Jun 2016

SLEEPY EYES CHUCK TODD

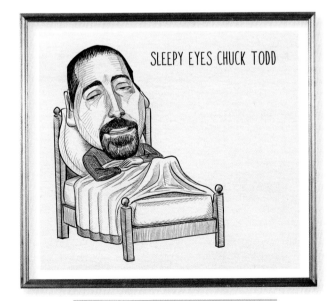

LYIN' TED

Donald J. Trump
@realDonaldTrump
Following

Lyin' Ted Cruz denied that he had anything to do with the G.Q. model photo post of Melania. That's why we call him Lyin' Ted!

10:22 AM - 23 Mar 2016

Donald J. Trump
@realDonaldTrump
Following

Word is that Sleepy Eyes Chuck Todd, who has failed so badly with Meet the Press, will be taking over for now irrelevant Brian Williams!

6:54 PM - 7 Feb 2015 from Palm Beach, FL

> **Donald J. Trump** ✓
> @realDonaldTrump ✓ Following
>
> Low energy Jeb Bush just endorsed a man he truly hates, Lyin' Ted Cruz. Honestly, I can't blame Jeb in that I drove him into oblivion!
>
> 12:49 PM · 23 Mar 2016

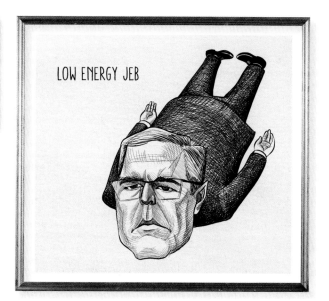

LOW ENERGY JEB

> **Donald J. Trump** ✓
> @realDonaldTrump ✓ Following
>
> Truly weird Senator Rand Paul of Kentucky reminds me of a spoiled brat without a properly functioning brain. He was terrible at DEBATE!
>
> 5:41 PM · 10 Aug 2015 from Manhattan, NY

TRULY WEIRD RAND PAUL

> **Donald J. Trump** ✓
> @realDonaldTrump ✓ Following
>
> I heard poorly rated @Morning_Joe speaks badly of me (don't watch anymore). Then how come low I.Q. Crazy Mika, along with Psycho Joe, came..
>
> 5:52 AM · 29 Jun 2017

PSYCHO JOE & LOW I.Q. MIKA

SNEAKY DIANNE FEINSTEIN

> **Donald J. Trump** ✓
> @realDonaldTrump ✓ Following
>
> The fact that Sneaky Dianne Feinstein, who has on numerous occasions stated that collusion between Trump/Russia has not been found, would release testimony in such an underhanded and possibly illegal way, totally without authorization, is a disgrace. Must have tough Primary!
>
> 10:00 AM · 10 Jan 2018

CRAZY BERNIE

Donald J. Trump ✔
@realDonaldTrump
Following

Michael Wolff is a total loser who made up stories in order to sell this really boring and untruthful book. He used Sloppy Steve Bannon, who cried when he got fired and begged for his job. Now Sloppy Steve has been dumped like a dog by almost everyone. Too bad!

11:32 PM - 5 Jan 2018

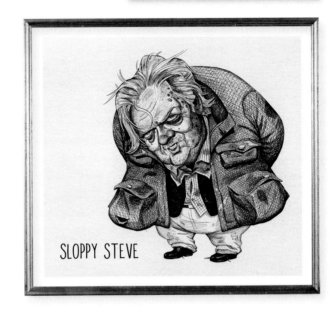

SLOPPY STEVE

Donald J. Trump ✔
@realDonaldTrump
Following

I don't want to hit Crazy Bernie Sanders too hard yet because I love watching what he is doing to Crooked Hillary. His time will come!

6:26 AM - 11 May 2016

Donald J. Trump ✔
@realDonaldTrump
Following

Just heard Foreign Minister of North Korea speak at U.N. If he echoes thoughts of Little Rocket Man, they won't be around much longer!

11:08 PM - 23 Sep 2017

LITTLE ROCKET MAN

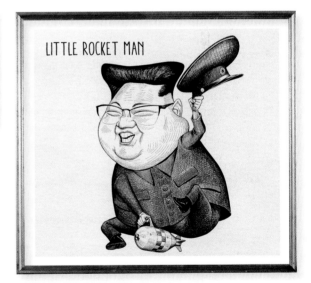

CRYIN' CHUCK SCHUMER

Donald J. Trump ✔
@realDonaldTrump
Following

Cryin' Chuck Schumer stated recently, "I do not have confidence in him (James Comey) any longer." Then acts so indignant. #draintheswamp

7:42 PM - 9 May 2017

SAD!: A RETROSPECTIVE

The many people, events, and twists of fate that made Donald Trump feel this human emotion

Donald J. Trump
@realDonaldTrump

Democrat Congresswoman totally fabricated what I said to the wife of a soldier who died in action (and I have proof). Sad!

7:25 AM - 18 Oct 2017

Donald J. Trump
@realDonaldTrump

My son Donald did a good job last night. He was open, transparent and innocent. This is the greatest Witch Hunt in political history. Sad!

6:19 AM - 12 Jul 2017

Donald J. Trump
@realDonaldTrump

The election is absolutely being rigged by the dishonest and distorted media pushing Crooked Hillary - but also at many polling places - SAD

1:01 PM - 16 Oct 2016

Donald J. Trump
@realDonaldTrump

The Democrats have said some of the worst things about James Comey, including the fact that he should be fired, but now they play so sad!

7:10 AM - 10 May 2017

Donald J. Trump
@realDonaldTrump
Following

Putin has become a big hero in Russia with an all time high popularity. Obama, on the other hand, has fallen to his lowest ever numbers. SAD

10:00 PM - 21 Mar 2014

Donald J. Trump
@realDonaldTrump
Following

FAKE NEWS media knowingly doesn't tell the truth. A great danger to our country. The failing @nytimes has become a joke. Likewise @CNN. Sad!

10:09 PM - 24 Feb 2017

Donald J. Trump
@realDonaldTrump
Following

.@ArsenioHall - How quickly people forget, but not me! You told me that without The Apprentice you could never have gotten your show - Sad!

12:06 PM - 29 Mar 2014

Donald J. Trump
@realDonaldTrump
Following

The United Nations has such great potential but right now it is just a club for people to get together, talk and have a good time. So sad!

1:41 PM - 26 Dec 2016

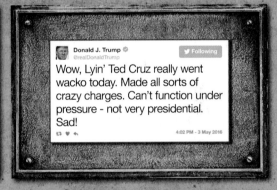

Donald J. Trump
@realDonaldTrump
Following

Wow, Lyin' Ted Cruz really went wacko today. Made all sorts of crazy charges. Can't function under pressure - not very presidential. Sad!

4:02 PM - 3 May 2016

Donald J. Trump
@realDonaldTrump
Following

After 7 months of investigations & committee hearings about my "collusion with the Russians," nobody has been able to show any proof. Sad!

4:53 AM - 16 Jun 2017

Donald J. Trump
@realDonaldTrump
Following

Because of me, the Republican Party has taken in millions of new voters, a record. If they are not careful, they will all leave. Sad!

7:05 PM - 2 Mar 2016

THE WORLD ACCORDING TO TRUMP

★

DONALD TRUMP'S MAKING PLACES GREAT AGAIN DOESN'T STOP WITH AMERICA. SEE WHAT THE CURRENT PRESIDENT OF THE UNITED STATES HAS TWEETED ABOUT OTHER COUNTRIES TO RE-GREATEN THEM AGAIN, TOO.

U.S.

CANADA

UNITED STATES

MEXICO

CUBA

COLOMBIA

★ THE AMERICAS ★

Donald J. Trump @
@realDonaldTrump

Canada has made business for
our dairy farmers in Wisconsin and
other border states very difficult.
We will not stand for this. Watch!

8:30 AM - 25 Apr 2017

Donald J. Trump @
@realDonaldTrump

The Mexican legal system is
corrupt, as is much of Mexico. Pay
me the money that is owed me
now - and stop sending criminals
over our border

7:47 PM - 24 Feb 2015 from Manhattan, NY

Donald J. Trump @
@realDonaldTrump

If Cuba is unwilling to make a better
deal for the Cuban people, the
Cuban/American people and the
U.S. as a whole, I will terminate
deal.

9:02 AM - 28 Nov 2016

Donald J. Trump @
@realDonaldTrump

Can you believe it—the model who
mysteriously disappeared from the
ObamaCare website is not a US
citizen—she's from Colombia.

10:03 AM - 13 Nov 2013

RUSSIA

SWEDEN

UNITED
KINGDOM

GERMANY

FRANCE

ITALY

GREECE

★ EUROPE ★

Donald J. Trump @realDonaldTrump 🐦 Following

Remember when I recently said that Brussels is a "hell hole" and a mess and the failing @nytimes wrote a critical article. I was so right!

10:17 AM - 24 Mar 2016

Donald J. Trump @realDonaldTrump 🐦 Following

I told you @TIME Magazine would never pick me as person of the year despite being the big favorite They picked person who is ruining Germany

8:53 AM - 9 Dec 2015

Donald J. Trump @realDonaldTrump 🐦 Following

Sad. Our food stamp rolls now surpass the entire population of Spain http://bit.ly/Y5PzX5 We must do better or we will be Greece.

12:01 PM - 12 Feb 2013

Donald J. Trump @realDonaldTrump 🐦 Following

Top suspect in Paris massacre, Salah Abdeslam, who also knew of the Brussels attack, is no longer talking. Weak leaders, ridiculous laws!

10:43 PM - 25 Mar 2016

Donald J. Trump @realDonaldTrump 🐦 Following

Everyone should boycott Italy if Amanda Knox is not freed---she is totally innocent.

12:12 PM - 30 Sep 2011

Donald J. Trump @realDonaldTrump 🐦 Following

The United Kingdom is trying hard to disguise their massive Muslim problem. Everybody is wise to what is happening, very sad! Be honest.

7:49 AM - 10 Dec 2015

Donald J. Trump @realDonaldTrump 🐦 Following

First Minister @AlexSalmond will be destroying the beauty of Scotland with his insane desire for bird killing wind turbines.

3:48 PM - 9 Aug 2013

Donald J. Trump @realDonaldTrump 🐦 Following

Give the public a break - The FAKE NEWS media is trying to say that large scale immigration in Sweden is working out just beautifully. NOT!

9:15 AM - 20 Feb 2017

Donald J. Trump @realDonaldTrump 🐦 Following

Do you think Putin will be going to The Miss Universe Pageant in November in Moscow - if so, will he become my new best friend?

11:17 PM - 18 Jun 2013

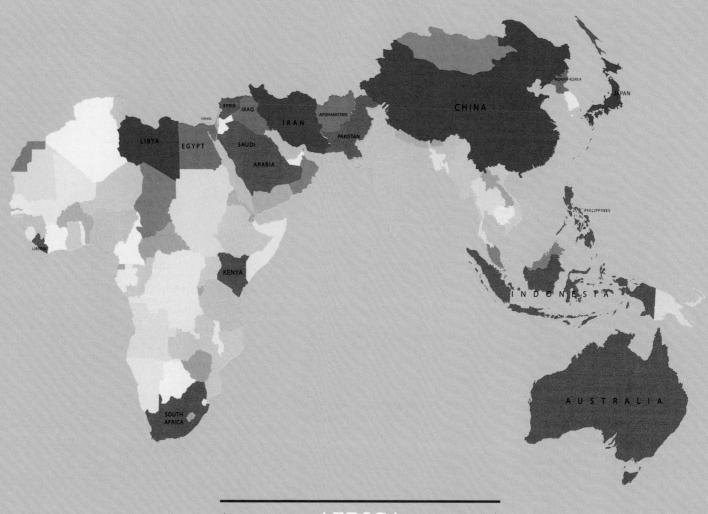

★ AFRICA ★

> **Donald J. Trump** ✔
> @realDonaldTrump
>
> Let's take a closer look at that birth certificate. @BarackObama was described in 2003 as being "born in Kenya."
>
> 3:31 PM · 18 May 2012

> **Donald J. Trump** ✔
> @realDonaldTrump
>
> Obama won't send troops to fight jihadists, yet sends them to Liberia to contract Ebola. He is a delusional failure.
>
> 4:49 PM · 9 Oct 2014

> **Donald J. Trump** ✔
> @realDonaldTrump
>
> I always said the people we fought for in Libya were bad news. Once again, I was right.
>
> 2:40 PM · 12 Sep 2012

ALL OF WEST AFRICA (and also sort of ISRAEL)

> **Donald J. Trump** ✔
> @realDonaldTrump
>
> As I have long been saying, South Africa is a total - and very dangerous - mess. Just watch the evening news (when not talking weather).
>
> 7:03 PM · 20 Apr 2015

> **Donald J. Trump** ✔
> @realDonaldTrump
>
> President Obama, I have an idea! Pretend that West Africa is Israel and then you will be able to stop the Ebola area flights.
>
> 11:21 PM · 4 Oct 2014

MIDDLE EAST

Donald J. Trump @realDonaldTrump · Following

Afghanistan is a total disaster. We don't know what we are doing. They are, in addition to everything else, robbing us blind.

2:17 PM - 12 Mar 2012

Donald J. Trump @realDonaldTrump · Following

Iran continues to delay the nuclear deal while doing many bad things behind our backs. Time to WALK and double the sanctions. Stop payments!

9:25 AM - 10 Jul 2015 from Beverly Hills, CA

Donald J. Trump @realDonaldTrump · Following

Iraq in political turmoil one day after we leave---I told you so.

9:22 AM - 20 Dec 2011

Donald J. Trump @realDonaldTrump · Following

With allies like Egypt and Libya, who needs enemies?!

1:13 PM - 13 Sep 2012

Donald J. Trump @realDonaldTrump · Following

When will Pakistan apologize to us for providing safe sanctuary to Osama Bin Laden for 6 years?! Some "ally."

4:22 PM - 5 Jul 2012

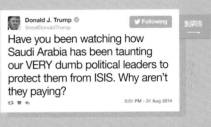

Donald J. Trump @realDonaldTrump · Following

Have you been watching how Saudi Arabia has been taunting our VERY dumb political leaders to protect them from ISIS. Why aren't they paying?

5:51 PM - 31 Aug 2014

Donald J. Trump @realDonaldTrump · Following

If we are going to continue to be stupid and go into Syria (watch Russia), as they say in the movies, SHOOT FIRST AND TALK LATER!

8:19 AM - 29 Aug 2013

ASIA / PACIFIC

Donald J. Trump @realDonaldTrump · Following

Wake Up America -- China is eating our lunch.

10:36 AM - 3 Aug 2011

Donald J. Trump @realDonaldTrump · Following

In debate, @MittRomney should ask Obama why autobiography states "born in Kenya, raised in Indonesia."

3:21 PM - 1 Oct 2012

Donald J. Trump @realDonaldTrump · Following

Does President Obama ever discuss the sneak attack on Pearl Harbor while he's in Japan? Thousands of American lives lost. #MDW

5:34 PM - 28 May 2016

Donald J. Trump @realDonaldTrump · Following

Crazy Dennis Rodman is saying I wanted to go to North Korea with him. Never discussed, no interest, last place on Earth I want to go to.

9:34 PM - 7 May 2014

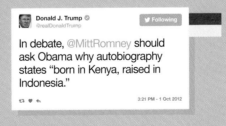

Donald J. Trump @realDonaldTrump · Following

China wouldn't provide a red carpet stairway from Air Force One and then Philippines President calls Obama "the son of a whore." Terrible!

7:12 AM - 6 Sep 2016

Donald J. Trump @realDonaldTrump · Following

Do you believe it? The Obama Administration agreed to take thousands of illegal immigrants from Australia. Why? I will study this dumb deal!

10:55 PM - 1 Feb 2017

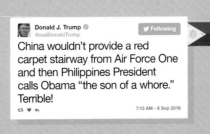

TRUMP VS. TRUMP

Most politicians base their decisions on strongly held beliefs. President Trump's brain is so uniquely good (or great) that it can hold many different beliefs on the same subject. This is an amazing, beautiful gift. Or it isn't. Or it's both.

★ **THE ELECTORAL COLLEGE** ★

Donald J. Trump ✔
@realDonaldTrump
🐦 Following

The electoral college is a disaster for a democracy.

11:45 PM - 6 Nov 2012

Donald J. Trump ✔
@realDonaldTrump
🐦 Following

The Electoral College is actually genius in that it brings all states, including the smaller ones, into play. Campaigning is much different!

8:40 AM - 15 Nov 2016

★ **POST-ELECTION PROTESTS** ★

Donald J. Trump ✔
@realDonaldTrump
🐦 Following

We can't let this happen. We should march on Washington and stop this travesty. Our nation is totally divided!

11:29 PM - 6 Nov 2012

Donald J. Trump ✔
@realDonaldTrump
🐦 Following

Just had a very open and successful presidential election. Now professional protesters, incited by the media, are protesting. Very unfair!

9:19 PM - 10 Nov 2016

★ MARCO RUBIO ★

> **Donald J. Trump** ✔
> @realDonaldTrump
> 🐦 Following
>
> Marco Rubio is being crucified by the media for drinking water during speech!
>
> ⟲ ♥ ↰   1:58 PM - 13 Feb 2013

> **Donald J. Trump** ✔
> @realDonaldTrump
> 🐦 Following
>
> Marco Rubio couldn't even respond properly to President Obama's State of the Union Speech without pouring sweat & chugging water. He choked!
>
> ⟲ ♥ ↰   10:37 PM - 9 Nov 2015

★ SYRIA ★

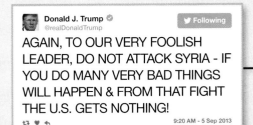

> **Donald J. Trump** ✔
> @realDonaldTrump
> 🐦 Following
>
> AGAIN, TO OUR VERY FOOLISH LEADER, DO NOT ATTACK SYRIA - IF YOU DO MANY VERY BAD THINGS WILL HAPPEN & FROM THAT FIGHT THE U.S. GETS NOTHING!
>
> ⟲ ♥ ↰   9:20 AM - 5 Sep 2013

> **Donald J. Trump** ✔
> @realDonaldTrump
> 🐦 Following
>
> Congratulations to our great military men and women for representing the United States, and the world, so well in the Syria attack.
>
> ⟲ ♥ ↰   10:54 AM - 8 Apr 2017

★ GOLF ★

> **Donald J. Trump** ✔
> @realDonaldTrump
> 🐦 Following
>
> Can you believe that,with all of the problems and difficulties facing the U.S., President Obama spent the day playing golf.Worse than Carter
>
> ⟲ ♥ ↰   8:03 PM - 13 Oct 2014

> **Donald J. Trump** ✔
> @realDonaldTrump
> 🐦 Following
>
> Played golf today with Prime Minister Abe of Japan and @TheBig_Easy, Ernie Els, and had a great time. Japan is very well represented!
>
> ⟲ ♥ ↰   6:15 PM - 11 Feb 2017

VS.

★ TIME MAGAZINE ★

Donald J. Trump ✓
@realDonaldTrump
🐦 Following

The Time Magazine list of the 100 Most Influential People is a joke and stunt of a magazine that will, like Newsweek,soon be dead. Bad list!

11:54 PM - 26 Apr 2013

Donald J. Trump ✓
@realDonaldTrump
🐦 Following

Thank you to Time Magazine and Financial Times for naming me "Person of the Year" - a great honor!

8:09 AM - 15 Dec 2016

★ ANONYMOUS SOURCES ★

Donald J. Trump ✓
@realDonaldTrump
🐦 Following

An 'extremely credible source' has called my office and told me that @BarackObama's birth certificate is a fraud.

4:23 PM - 6 Aug 2012

Donald J. Trump ✓
@realDonaldTrump
🐦 Following

Remember, don't believe "sources said" by the VERY dishonest media. If they don't name the sources, the sources don't exist.

8:50 AM - 30 Sep 2016

★ MEETING WITH NORTH KOREA ★

Donald J. Trump ✓
@realDonaldTrump
🐦 Following

I told Rex Tillerson, our wonderful Secretary of State, that he is wasting his time trying to negotiate with Little Rocket Man…

10:30 AM - 1 Oct 2017

Donald J. Trump ✓
@realDonaldTrump
🐦 Following

The deal with North Korea is very much in the making and will be, if completed, a very good one for the World. Time and place to be determined.

7:42 PM - 9 Mar 2018

★　**OBAMACARE**　★

Donald J. Trump ✓
@realDonaldTrump
🐦 Following

Republicans should just REPEAL failing ObamaCare now & work on a new Healthcare Plan that will start from a clean slate. Dems will join in!

10:17 PM - 17 Jul 2017

Donald J. Trump ✓
@realDonaldTrump
🐦 Following

As I have always said, let ObamaCare fail and then come together and do a great healthcare plan. Stay tuned!

7:58 AM - 18 Jul 2017

★　**WATCHING TV**　★

Donald J. Trump ✓
@realDonaldTrump
🐦 Following

The W.H. is functioning perfectly, focused on HealthCare, Tax Cuts/Reform & many other things. I have very little time for watching T.V.

9:39 AM - 12 Jul 2017

Donald J. Trump ✓
@realDonaldTrump
🐦 Following

I am watching @FoxNews and how fairly they are treating me and my words, and @CNN, and the total distortion of my words and what I am saying

11:08 AM - 13 Jun 2016

Donald J. Trump ✓
@realDonaldTrump
🐦 Following

Watched low rated @Morning_Joe for first time in long time. FAKE NEWS. He called me to stop a National Enquirer article. I said no! Bad show

7:55 AM - 30 Jun 2017

Donald J. Trump ✓
@realDonaldTrump
🐦 Following

Heading back to Washington after working hard and watching some of the worst and most dishonest Fake News reporting I have ever seen!

6:22 PM - 20 Aug 2017

Donald J. Trump ✓
@realDonaldTrump
🐦 Following

I love watching these poor, pathetic people (pundits) on television working so hard and so seriously to try and figure me out. They can't!

7:43 AM - 12 Aug 2016

Donald J. Trump ✓
@realDonaldTrump
🐦 Following

I look forward to watching @megynkelly tonight, 8 PM ET. It will be interesting to see how she treats me—I think she will be very fair.

11:25 AM - 17 May 2016

Elements!!! of STYLE
POETICS OF A PRESIDENT

"nobody, not even the rain, has such small hands" —E.E. CUMMINGS

In the right hands, tweets are poems—pure expression, distilled and refined into elegant written word. Best do-er of this: TRUMP.

Like the man himself, Trump's style has time for neither rules nor decency. His grammar is rebellious. His syntax, beyond rules. His rhythm, cavemanlike. But this primal simplicity is exactly how Trump captivates. It's chaos. Seemingly pointless exclamation points subdivide parentheticals that sit inside acronyms that don't even exist. He Capitalizes at random, sometimes for emphasis, Sometimes not. And throughout, the work vibrates with outbursts of emotional intensity: stark despair ("SAD!"), sympathetic joy ("CONGRATS!"), impotent rage ("NO COLLUSION!").

Unorthodox? MAGA. But Trump still does what all great poets do—compel their readers to question. Why did he put quotation marks around the word "me"? How could anyone misspell the word "tap"? What, for the love of all in this world that is holy, is up with this guy? These are the eternal mysteries that only poetry can answer.

The Trump Twitter Library's big, beautiful
MAGA-netic Poetry Wall of all the best words

THE NASTY ENEMY COMEY
FIRED # MAGA
DEAD PUPPET

11:50 AM - Jun 2017

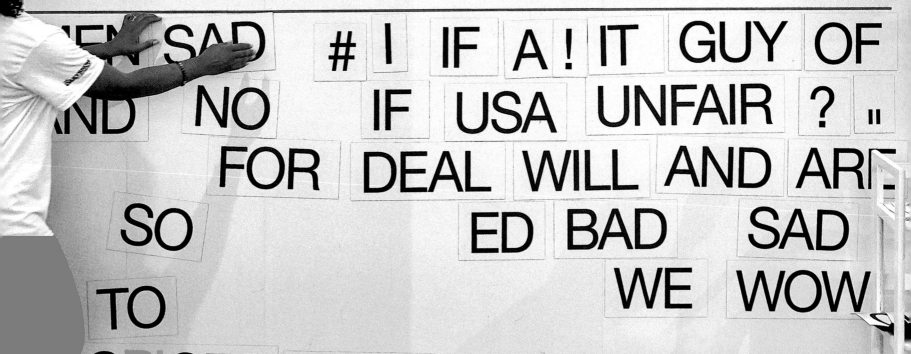

"COVFEFE"

31 MAY 2017 – 12:06 AM (DELETED APPROXIMATELY 5:45 AM)

MEDIUM: TWITTER FOR IPHONE

DIMENSIONS: 43 CHARACTERS

Here in his single-tweet Minimalist phase, the real subject is not Trump's wholly original non-word, but rather that which is not seen: the ghostly remainder of the sentence that would have followed. With confident reference to Gilbert Stuart's "Unfinished Portrait" of President Washington, President Trump compels viewers to a greater level of engagement, demanding that they fill the post-fragment negative space. Seeking guidance along this path not taken, we find ourselves shocked at how familiar we have become with his oeuvre—feeling, as a community, the unspoken "Sad!," the silent boast, the invisible #MAGA.

"NOBODY HAS MORE RESPECT"

15 OCT 2016 – 2:29 PM

MEDIUM: TWITTER FOR ANDROID

DIMENSIONS: 137 CHARACTERS

Beset on all sides by the *Access Hollywood* "Pussy Grab" tape and multiple accusations of sexual assault, Donald Trump is a candidate on the brink, pushed to the very limits of his character count. Forged during the darkest days of Trump's late Campaign Era, this tweet is a master parry intended to deny, deflect, and riposte—and it succeeds on all counts. As this tweet begins, America's concern is for his thirteen alleged victims, yet 137 characters later, there is concern for but one victim: Donald Trump. The true crime being committed is not sexual assault, but rather election theft. And then comes the ultimate denouement—"Nobody has more respect for women than me!"—a statement of climactic hyperbole that stuns the reader into submission. This is an artist who can, linguistically, do whatever he wants. "When you're a star, they let you do it." Indeed.

"COMPOSITION IN MEME AND BODYSLAM"

2 JULY 2017 – 9:21 AM

MEDIUM: TWITTER FOR IPHONE

DIMENSIONS: 18 CHARACTERS, 1280 X 720 VIDEO

Behold CNN, trapped eternally in a Sisyphean cycle of brutality and defeat. Trump's single-most retweeted work melds professional wrestling imagery and media criticism, translating his verbal assaults on America's press into pure preliterate spectacle: Warrior King Trump annihilating a faceless and pathetic CNN avatar in visceral, visual terms that even a toddler could grasp. Released on July 4th weekend, "Bodyslam" is itself an historic declaration, not just of the President's independence, but of his honor, dignity, and comfort with casual violence.

CURATOR'S NOTE: *Scholars later reattributed this as a "found art" piece, based on the work of Reddit user "HanAssholeSolo," which Trump, in a brilliant act of Duchampian appropriation, copied and pasted.*

"MY BUTTON WORKS"

2 JAN 2018 – 7:49 PM

MEDIUM: TWITTER FOR IPHONE

DIMENSIONS: 280 CHARACTERS

Created near the end of his "President of the United States" period's first year, "My Button Works" was Trump's response to a piece by the "bad boy" of North Korea's Nuclear Realist school, Kim Jong-un. We watch in awe as Trump walks an atomic tightrope like it was a nonchalant stroll down a Tuesday morning fairway, first taunting the nuclear-armed Kim, and then showing his skill for fresh diplomatic thinking with his subtle use of the magic word "please."

But there remains the central enigma. Trump seems to speak of a literal "Nuclear Button," when as he and the rest of everyone knows, there is no such thing, and even if there were, its physical size would have nothing to do with anything. The result is a dreamy phantasmagoria so befuddling that, by tweet's end, observers can no longer distinguish between madman and truth-teller, between thoughtless belligerence and canny statecraft, or between a global nuclear apocalypse and a giant dong competition.

"VERY STABLE GENIUS"

6 JAN 2018 – 7:19 AM, 7:27 AM, 7:30 AM

MEDIUM: TWITTER FOR IPHONE

DIMENSIONS: 414 CHARACTERS

Among Western art's proudest traditions is the psychologically probing self-portrait. We think of Van Gogh's oils speaking deeper emotional truths than words ever could. We think of Rembrandt bearing humble witness to his, and our, tragic mortality. And now we think of Donald Trump, whose stunning Twitter triptych "Very Stable Genius" dared to express *his* truth, even when he had ample reason to think literally no one would believe him. Along with that 1970s hotel-bed bathrobe photo, it is Trump's bravest work of self-exposure.

The work unfolds across three panels. The first comprises a brisk, classicist "hoax/lapdog/Fake News" dismissal narrative. Then Trump swivels to the cautionary tale of Crooked Hillary Clinton, whose impudent questioning of his, like, really smartness led to her fiery demise. The work now transfigures into almost pointillist autobiography, as powerful mogul metamorphosizes into world leader (on first try). But it is Trump's third-panel conclusion that still amazes—a statement of self-identity so bold, so definitive, it has forever redefined the concepts of "stable," and "genius," and probably even "very."

For further insight into the making of "Very Stable Genius," please turn the page.

Though Secret Service protocols prevent the direct examination of Trump's brain as he writes a tweet, expert psycholinguists have here recreated the thought process behind one of the president's most complex compositions. As you will see, what first appears to be an ungainly three-part rant about Russian collusion, media bias, and mental fitness is in actuality the product of 100 billion of the world's best neurons making thousands of terrific micro-decisions.

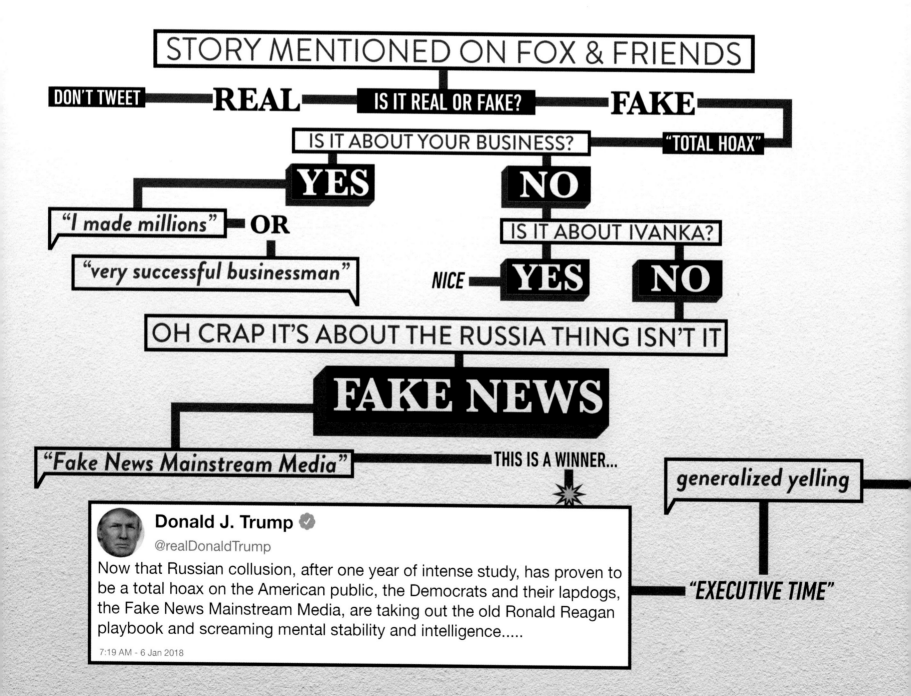

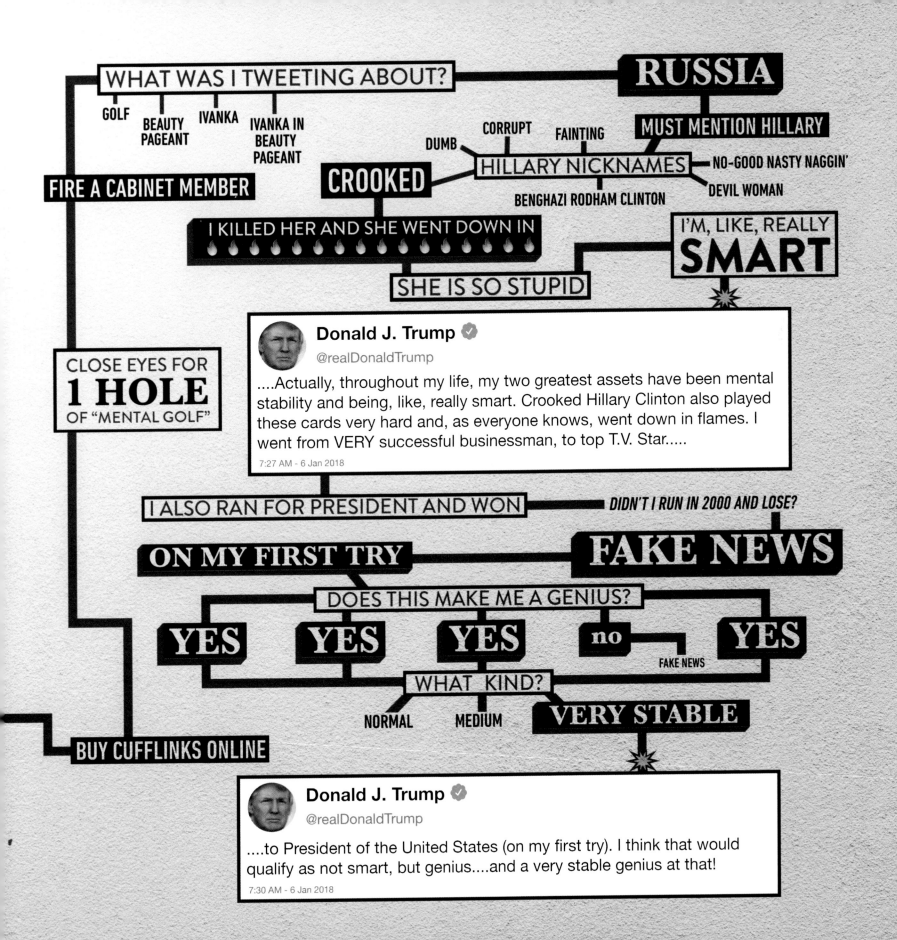

HALL OF RETWEETS

It is indisputable that history will know Donald Trump mainly for his selflessness. A prime example was his generous use of Twitter's "retweet" function. While his own tweets always garner the most praise, attention, and then more praise, Trump's retweets often raise the voices of those whom society has, for some reason, tried really hard to silence.

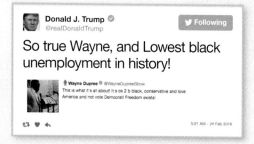

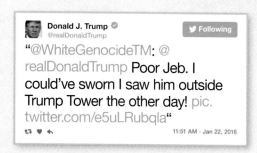

JACK POSOBIEC
After days of absorbing unfair criticism of his claim that a white nationalist rally had "very fine people on both sides," Trump takes to Twitter to show by retweeting that some folks liked his comments. Was the man Trump retweeted an accused supporter of white nationalists who had promoted the thoroughly debunked, objectively nutbag "Pizzagate" conspiracy theory? Sure, maybe, but the more important point is, the president probably didn't know this, so what he did was fine.

SANDY HOOK TRUTHER
The fact that this Trump retweet's original author had called the Sandy Hook Elementary School shooting a "hoax" has nothing to do with Mr. Trump, and on analysis it is really not a problem.

TRUMP RETWEETS @WhiteGenocideTM
After this retweet, many desperate Trump haters tried to read something into the name of Twitter user @WhiteGenocideTM, but this seems like a stretch. In point of fact, Trump doing this was okay.

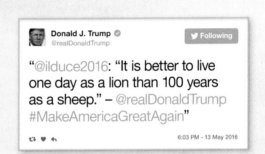

FAKE BLACK/WHITE CRIME STATS

Ever the canny politician, Trump retweets a fictional organization's made-up, widely debunked statistics that make his case for interracial fear and animosity better than accurate ones would have. Normal stuff that isn't a big deal.

MUSSOLINI QUOTE

When the fake news tried to shame Trump for retweeting a quote from Italian fascist leader/Hitler pal Benito Mussolini, Trump turned the tables, telling Sleepy Eyes Chuck Todd, "It was a very good quote. An interesting quote." Pressed on whether he wanted to be associated with fascism, Trump replied, "I want to be associated with interesting quotes." Checkmate, MSM. Plus, anyway, it was fine.

RT @TRUMPISM_45 @REALDONALDTRUMP WE WON. MOVE ON.

As this Twitter user noted, Donald Trump did win. Could Trump have found and retweeted this same point made by someone who hadn't also claimed that Hillary Clinton had committed murder to cover up her other crimes? Why engage in hypotheticals? Besides, doing this was okay.

"WE BUILD TOO MANY WALLS AND NOT ENOUGH BRIDGES." - ISAAC NEWTON
12 MAY 2009

DONALD J. TRUMP @REALDONALDTRUMP
SECURE THE BORDER! BUILD A WALL!
4:11 PM - 7 OCT 2013

DONALD J. TRUMP @REALDONALDTRUMP
THE FIGHT AGAINST ISIS STARTS AT OUR BORDER. 'AT LEAST' 10 ISIS HAVE BEEN CAUGHT CROSSING THE MEXICO BORDER. BUILD A WALL!
4:34 PM - 5 OCT 2014

DONALD J. TRUMP @REALDONALDTRUMP
MEXICO'S COURT SYSTEM... WANT NOTHING TO DO W... MEXICO OTHER THAN TO... IMPENETRABLE WALL AN... THEM FROM RIPPING OFF...

DONALD J. TRUMP @REALDONALDTRUMP
WE MUST BUILD A WALL TO SECURE OUR BORDER. IT WILL SAVE LIVES AND HELP MAKE AMERICA GREAT AGAIN!
9:40 AM - 14 JUL 2015
3:44 PM - 27 JUL 2015

DONALD J. TRUMP @REALDONALDTRUMP
A NATION WITHOUT BORDERS IS NOT A NATION AT ALL. WE MUST HAVE A WALL. THE RULE OF LAW MATTERS. JEB JUST DOESN'T GET IT.
5:20 PM - 28 JUL 2015

DONALD J. TRUMP @REALDONALDTRUMP
AGAIN, ILLEGAL IMMIGRANT IS CHARGED WITH THE FATAL BLUDGEONING OF A WONDERFUL AND LOVED 64 YEAR OLD WOMAN. GET THEM OUT AND BUILD A WALL!
8:29 PM - 10 AUG 2015

DONALD J. TRUMP @REALDONALDTRUMP
WE MUST BUILD A GREAT WALL BETWEEN MEXICO AND THE UNITED STATES!
5:49 PM - 1 APR 2016

DONALD J. TRUMP @REALDONALDTRUMP
OBAMA SAYS A WALL AT OUR SOUTHERN BORDER WON'T ENHANCE OUR SECURITY (WRONG) AND YET HE NOW WANTS TO BUILD A MUCH BIGGER WALL (FENCE) AT W.H.
6:41 AM - 30 MAY 2016

DONALD J. TRUMP @REALDONALDTRUMP
IN GETTING THE ENDORSEMENT OF THE 16,500 BORDER PATROL AGENTS (THANK YOU), THE STATEMENT WAS MADE THAT THE WALL WAS VERY NECESSARY!
7:00 AM - 30 MAY 2016

DONALD J. TRUMP @REALDONALDTRUMP
NEW GOP PLATFORM NO... INCLUDES LANGUAGE T... SUPPORTS THE BORDER... WE WILL BUILD THE WA... MAKE AMERICA SAFE A...
5:56 PM

DONALD J. TRUMP @REALDONALDTRUMP — PART 1 OF 2
...ING THAT THE GREAT BORDER ...L COST MORE THAN THE ...ENT ORIGINALLY THOUGHT, ...E NOT GOTTEN INVOLVED IN
8:18 AM - 11 FEB 2017

DONALD J. TRUMP @REALDONALDTRUMP — PART 2 OF 2
...DESIGN OR NEGOTIATIONS YET. WHEN I DO, JUST LIKE WITH THE F-35 FIGHTERJET OR THE AIR FORCE ONE PROGRAM, PRICE WILL COME WAY DOWN!
8:18 AM - 11 FEB 2017

DONALD J. TRUMP @REALDONALDTRUMP
THE DEMOCRATS DON'T WANT MONEY FROM BUDGET GOING TO BORDER WALL DESPITE THE FACT THAT IT WILL STOP DRUGS AND VERY BAD MS 13 GANG MEMBERS.
11:42 AM - 23 APR 2017

DONALD J. TRUMP @REALDONALDTRUMP
EVENTUALLY, BUT AT A LATER DATE SO WE CAN GET STARTED EARLY, MEXICO WILL BE PAYING, IN SOME FORM, FOR THE BADLY NEEDED BORDER WALL.
11:44 AM - 23 APR 2017

DONALD J. TRUMP @REALDONALDTRUMP
THE WALL, WHICH IS ALREADY UNDER CONSTRUCTION IN THE FORM OF NEW RENOVATION OF OLD AND EXISTING FENCES AND WALLS, WILL CONTINUE TO BE BUILT.
6:20 AM - 14 SEP 2017

DONALD J. TRUMP @REALDONALDTRUMP
THE DEMOCRATS WANT MASSIVE TAX INCREASES & SOFT, CRIME PRODUCING BORDERS. THE REPUBLICANS WANT THE BIGGEST TAX CUT IN HISTORY & THE WALL!
6:36 AM - 11 OCT 2017

DONALD J. TRUMP @REALDONALDTRUMP
BORDER WALL PROTOTYPES UNDERWAY! <VIDEO>
7:03 AM - 17 OCT 2017

DONALD J. TRUMP @REALDONALDTRUMP
BORDER PATROL OFFICER... SOUTHERN BORDER, AND... BADLY HURT. WE WILL SE... AND BRING TO JUSTICE T... RESPONSIBLE. WE WILL, ... BUILD THE WALL!
8:29 P...

DONALD J. TRUMP @REALDONALDTRUMP — PART 1 OF 2
THE WALL, IT HAS NEVER CHANGED FROM THE FIRST DAY I CONCEIVED ...WILL BE, OF NECESSITY, SEE ...D IT WAS NEVER INTENDED TO BE ...AS WHERE THERE IS NATURAL ...SUCH AS MOUNTAINS, WASTELANDS ...VERS OR WATER.....
6:15 AM - 18 JAN 2018

DONALD J. TRUMP @REALDONALDTRUMP — PART 2 OF 2
...THE WALL WILL BE PAID FOR DIRECTLY OR INDIRECTLY, OR THROUGH ... TERM REIMBURSEMENT, BY MEXI... CH HAS A RIDICULOUS $71 BILLION DO... TRADE SURPLUS WITH THE U.S. THE $20 BI... LLAR WALL IS "PEANUTS" COMPARED ... ICO MAKES FROM THE U.S. NAFTA !...
18 JAN 2018

DONALD J. TRUMP @REALDONALDTRUMP
WE NEED THE WALL FOR THE SAFETY AND SECURITY OF OUR COUNTRY. WE NEED THE WALL TO HELP STOP THE MASSIVE INFLOW OF DRUGS FROM MEXICO, NOW RATED THE NUMBER ONE MOST DANGEROUS COUNTRY IN THE WORLD. IF THERE IS NO WALL, THERE IS NO DEAL!
8:16 AM - 18 JAN 2018

DONALD J. TRUMP @REALDONALDTRUMP
CRYIN' CHUCK SCHUMER FULLY UNDERSTANDS, ESPECIALLY AFTER HIS HUMILIATING DEFEAT, THAT IF THERE IS NO WALL, THERE IS NO DACA. WE MUST HAVE SAFETY AND SECURITY, TOGETHER WITH A STRONG MILITARY, FOR OUR GREAT PEOPLE!
11:07 PM - 23 JAN 2018

DONALD J. TRUMP @REALDONALDTRUMP
DACA WAS ABANDONED BY THE DEMOCRATS. VERY UNFAIR TO THEM! WOULD HAVE BEEN TIED TO DESPERATELY NEEDED WALL.
8:26 AM - 23 MAR 2018

...ERING A VETO OF THE OMNIBUS ...LL BASED ON THE FACT THAT THE ...S DACA RECIPIENTS HAVE BEEN ...ABANDONED BY THE DEMOCRATS (NOT ...ENTIONED IN BILL) AND THE BORDER WALL, ...S DESPERATELY NEEDED FOR OUR ...AL DEFENSE, IS NOT FULLY FUNDED.
8:55 AM - 23 MAR 2018

DONALD J. TRUMP @REALDONALDTRUMP
BECAUSE OF THE $700 & $716 BILLION DOLLARS GOTTEN TO REBUILD OUR MILITARY, MANY JOBS ARE CREATED AND OUR MILITARY IS AGAIN RICH. BUILDING A GREAT BORDER WALL, WITH DRUGS (POISON) AND ENEMY COMBATANTS POURING INTO OUR COUNTRY, IS ALL ABOUT NATIONAL DEFENSE. BUILD WALL THROUGH M!
6:33 AM - 25 MAR 2018

MUCH CAN BE DONE WITH THE $1,... GIVEN TO BUILDING AND FIXING T... WALL. IT IS JUST A DOWN PAYMEN... START IMMEDIATELY. THE REST OF... WILL COME - AND REMEMBER DAC... DEMOCRATS ABANDONED YOU (BU... NOT)!
6:42 AM

Since his 2015 Trump Tower escalator ride to destiny, the 45th president has had one main rallying cry: We have to build a wall. A simple promise from an extraordinarily simple man. The wall would be big. It would be strong. And Mexico would pay for it. Possibly "through reimbursement/other."

Many called the idea preposterous, but President Trump literally did not know the meaning of that word. And the reality is, bit by bit, Donald Trump has built a wall. A wall so big and strong, it is impenetrable to criticism, logic, or reason. It is a Wall of Tweets.

★ BY THE ★
NUMBERS*

*All data as of 22 May 2018. Because at some point you just have to stop.

GREAT

OVERRATED

NASCAR	MITT ROMNEY	MEGYN KELLY
RUSH LIMBAUGH	DENNIS RODMAN	"HAMILTON" SHOW
TOM BRADY	BILL CLINTON	CHER
ROBERT JEFFRESS	MARCO RUBIO	JERRY SEINFELD
ROGER AILES	MARK CUBAN	MERYL STREEP
STEVEN SPIELBERG	BARACK OBAMA	KARL ROVE
BREITBART	FOX NEWS	BUZZFEED
JENNIFER ANISTON	NEW YORK TIMES	HILLARY CLINTON
CHELSEA CLINTON	PAUL RYAN	SACHA BARON COHEN
HOWARD STERN	TED CRUZ	

OVERRATED
& GREAT

1 DAY
21 HOURS
56 MINUTES

LONGEST
TWITTER DROUGHT
SINCE ELECTED

"THIS CANNOT BE THE THE ACADEMY
AWARDS #OSCARS AWFUL!!!!!!!!!!!!!!!!" —2 Mar 2014

1 !!!!!!!!!!!!!!!!!
7 !!!!!!!!!!!
9 !!!!!!!!!
14 !!!!!!!
25 !!!!!!
58 !!!!!
147 !!!!
434 !!!
874 !!
14,928 !

CONSECUTIVE
" ! "

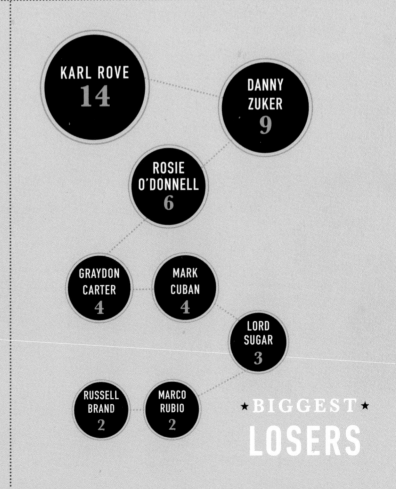

KARL ROVE
14

DANNY
ZUKER
9

ROSIE
O'DONNELL
6

GRAYDON
CARTER
4

MARK
CUBAN
4

LORD
SUGAR
3

RUSSELL
BRAND
2

MARCO
RUBIO
2

★ BIGGEST ★
LOSERS

★ FOX NEWS PERSONALITY ★
MENTIONS

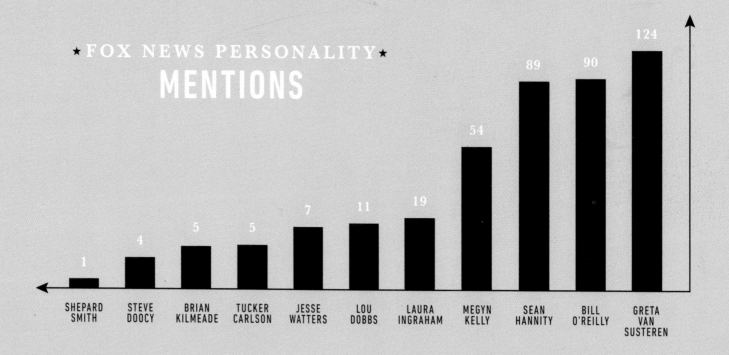

Name	Mentions
SHEPARD SMITH	1
STEVE DOOCY	4
BRIAN KILMEADE	5
TUCKER CARLSON	5
JESSE WATTERS	7
LOU DOBBS	11
LAURA INGRAHAM	19
MEGYN KELLY	54
SEAN HANNITY	89
BILL O'REILLY	90
GRETA VAN SUSTEREN	124

★ FAMILY ★
TWEETS

Name	Tweets
IVANKA	136
MELANIA	131
ERIC	104
DON JR	82
TIFFANY	6

★ MEDIA ★
MENTIONS

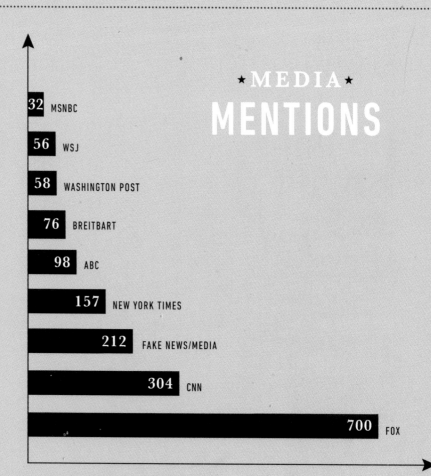

Outlet	Mentions
MSNBC	32
WSJ	56
WASHINGTON POST	58
BREITBART	76
ABC	98
NEW YORK TIMES	157
FAKE NEWS/MEDIA	212
CNN	304
FOX	700

"CROOKED HILLARY" 263
"LYIN' TED" 37
"GOOFY ELIZABETH WARREN" 23
"DOPEY SUGAR"* 21
"SLEEPY EYES CHUCK TODD" 18
"POCAHONTAS" 12
"LITTLE MARCO" 10
"CRAZY MEGYN" 8
"LOW ENERGY JEB" 7
"CRAZY BERNIE" 5
"CRYIN' CHUCK SCHUMER" 4

★TOP★
NICKNAMES

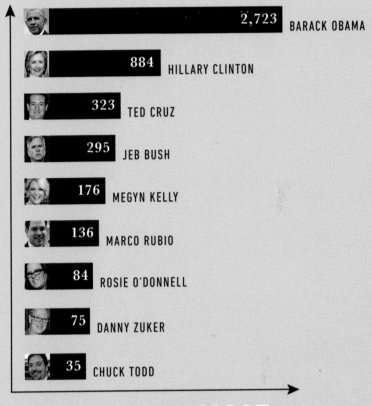

2,723	BARACK OBAMA
884	HILLARY CLINTON
323	TED CRUZ
295	JEB BUSH
176	MEGYN KELLY
136	MARCO RUBIO
84	ROSIE O'DONNELL
75	DANNY ZUKER
35	CHUCK TODD

★MOST★
ATTACKED

5

NUMBER OF
WHITE SUPREMACISTS
RETWEETED

DISHONORABLE MENTIONS:
3: LITTLE ROCKET MAN, LITTLE MORTY ZUCKERMAN
2: DOPEY JON STEWART, ROCKET MAN, LYIN' HILLARY, LIDDLE' BOB CORKER, LOW RATINGS JOE SCARBOROUGH, LIDDLE' ADAM SCHIFF, SLIPPERY JAMES COMEY, WACKY CONGRESSWOMAN WILSON, WACKY GLENN BECK, PELOSI/SCHUMER PUPPET JONES, CROOKED H FLUNKIE, WILD BILL, ANIMAL ASSAD
1: CHEATIN' OBAMA, CRAZY JOE SCARBOROUGH, PSYCHO JOE, CRAZY MIKA, DUMB AS A ROCK MIKA, FAKE TEARS CHUCK SCHUMER, CRAZY JOE BIDEN, AL FRANKENSTEIN, JEFF FLAKE(Y), FLAKE JEFF FLAKE, CRAZY JIM ACOSTA, LEAKIN' JAMES COMEY, LYING JAMES COMEY, SANCTIMONIOUS JAMES COMEY, SHADEY JAMES COMEY, SNEAKY DIANNE FEINSTEIN, CRYING GLENN BECK, FAILING GLENN BECK, DICKY DURBIN, SLEAZY ADAM SCHIFF, MR. MAGOO, MR. PEEPERS, DOPEY PRINCE, GOOFBALL ATHEIST PENN, SLOPPY MICHAEL MOORE
* REFERS TO BRITISH BILLIONAIRE AND BBC *APPRENTICE* HOST ALAN SUGAR

★ TWEETS ★
BY TIME OF DAY
SINCE BECOMING PRESIDENT

12

417   33

9   3

892   49

6

A.M.

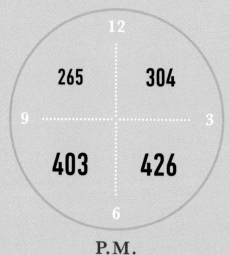

12

265   304

9   3

403   426

6

P.M.

BAD vs. SAD

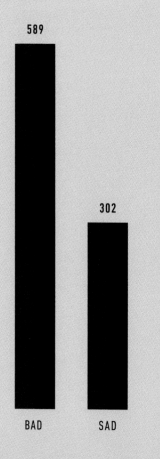

589

302

BAD   SAD

11

TWEET WITH FEWEST RETWEETS

"Enter the 'Think Like A Champion' signed book and keychain contest: http://www.trumpthinklikeachampion.com/contest/"

15 MAY 2009

TIFFANY vs. TIFFANY

6   6

DAUGHTER   STORE

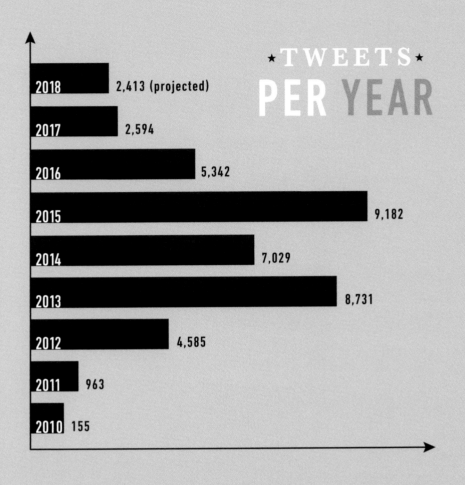

★ TWEETS ★
PER YEAR

Year	Tweets
2018	2,413 (projected)
2017	2,594
2016	5,342
2015	9,182
2014	7,029
2013	8,731
2012	4,585
2011	963
2010	155

2,344
OBAMA

MOST MENTIONED
OF ALL TIME

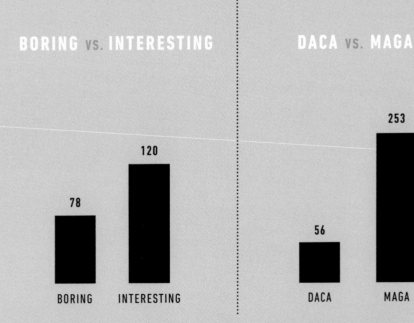

BORING VS. **INTERESTING**

78	120
BORING	INTERESTING

DACA VS. **MAGA**

56	253
DACA	MAGA

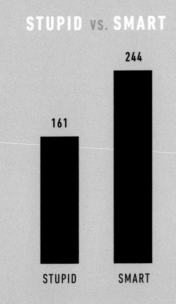

STUPID VS. **SMART**

161	244
STUPID	SMART

★ ★ ★

FEATURED COLLECTIONS

★ ★ ★

I'M THE BEST

★

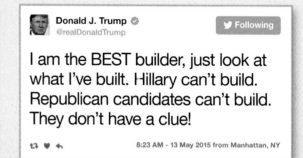

Donald J. Trump @realDonaldTrump · Following

Sorry losers and haters, but my I.Q. is one of the highest -and you all know it! Please don't feel so stupid or insecure,it's not your fault

9:37 PM - 8 May 2013

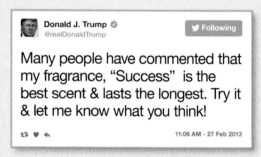

Donald J. Trump @realDonaldTrump · Following

I am the BEST builder, just look at what I've built. Hillary can't build. Republican candidates can't build. They don't have a clue!

8:23 AM - 13 May 2015 from Manhattan, NY

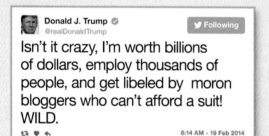

Donald J. Trump @realDonaldTrump · Following

Isn't it crazy, I'm worth billions of dollars, employ thousands of people, and get libeled by moron bloggers who can't afford a suit! WILD.

8:14 AM - 19 Feb 2014

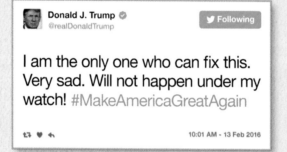

Donald J. Trump @realDonaldTrump · Following

I am the only one who can fix this. Very sad. Will not happen under my watch! #MakeAmericaGreatAgain

10:01 AM - 13 Feb 2016

Donald J. Trump @realDonaldTrump · Following

Many people have commented that my fragrance, "Success" is the best scent & lasts the longest. Try it & let me know what you think!

11:06 AM - 27 Feb 2013

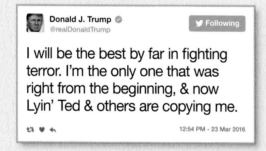

Donald J. Trump @realDonaldTrump · Following

I will be the best by far in fighting terror. I'm the only one that was right from the beginning, & now Lyin' Ted & others are copying me.

12:54 PM - 23 Mar 2016

Donald J. Trump @realDonaldTrump · Following

I started my business with very little and built it into a great company, with some of the best real estate assets in the World. Amazing!

11:08 AM - 27 Feb 2016

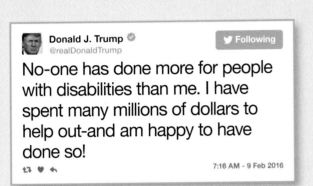

Donald J. Trump @realDonaldTrump — Following

No-one has done more for people with disabilities than me. I have spent many millions of dollars to help out-and am happy to have done so!

7:16 AM - 9 Feb 2016

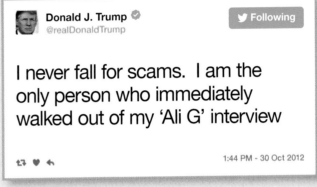

Donald J. Trump @realDonaldTrump — Following

I never fall for scams. I am the only person who immediately walked out of my 'Ali G' interview

1:44 PM - 30 Oct 2012

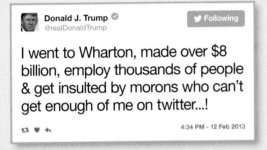

Donald J. Trump @realDonaldTrump — Following

I went to Wharton, made over $8 billion, employ thousands of people & get insulted by morons who can't get enough of me on twitter...!

4:34 PM - 12 Feb 2013

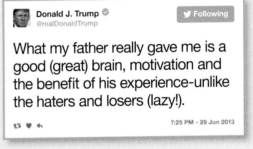

Donald J. Trump @realDonaldTrump — Following

What my father really gave me is a good (great) brain, motivation and the benefit of his experience-unlike the haters and losers (lazy!).

7:25 PM - 29 Jun 2013

Donald J. Trump @realDonaldTrump — Following

Nobody beats me on National Security.

1:06 PM - 8 Apr 2016

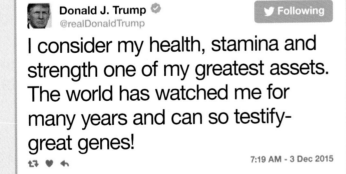

Donald J. Trump @realDonaldTrump — Following

I consider my health, stamina and strength one of my greatest assets. The world has watched me for many years and can so testify-great genes!

7:19 AM - 3 Dec 2015

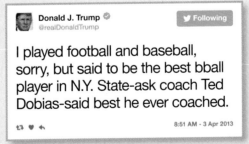

Donald J. Trump @realDonaldTrump — Following

I played football and baseball, sorry, but said to be the best bball player in N.Y. State-ask coach Ted Dobias-said best he ever coached.

8:51 AM - 3 Apr 2013

★ CONSTRUCTIVE CRITICISM ★

TRUMP TOWER'S LEAD REVIEWER SAVES AMERICA SOME TIME

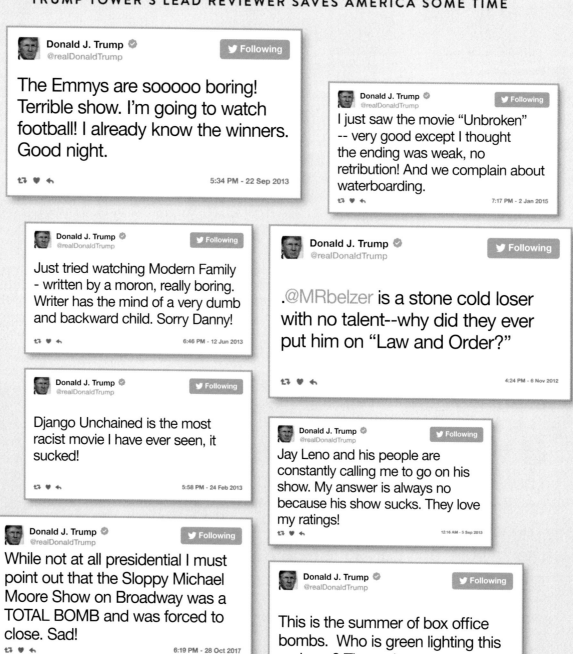

Donald J. Trump @realDonaldTrump — Following

The Emmys are sooooo boring! Terrible show. I'm going to watch football! I already know the winners. Good night.

5:34 PM - 22 Sep 2013

Donald J. Trump @realDonaldTrump — Following

I just saw the movie "Unbroken" -- very good except I thought the ending was weak, no retribution! And we complain about waterboarding.

7:17 PM - 2 Jan 2015

Donald J. Trump @realDonaldTrump — Following

Just tried watching Modern Family - written by a moron, really boring. Writer has the mind of a very dumb and backward child. Sorry Danny!

6:46 PM - 12 Jun 2013

Donald J. Trump @realDonaldTrump — Following

.@MRbelzer is a stone cold loser with no talent--why did they ever put him on "Law and Order?"

4:24 PM - 6 Nov 2012

Donald J. Trump @realDonaldTrump — Following

Django Unchained is the most racist movie I have ever seen, it sucked!

5:58 PM - 24 Feb 2013

Donald J. Trump @realDonaldTrump — Following

Jay Leno and his people are constantly calling me to go on his show. My answer is always no because his show sucks. They love my ratings!

12:16 AM - 5 Sep 2013

Donald J. Trump @realDonaldTrump — Following

While not at all presidential I must point out that the Sloppy Michael Moore Show on Broadway was a TOTAL BOMB and was forced to close. Sad!

6:19 PM - 28 Oct 2017

Donald J. Trump @realDonaldTrump — Following

This is the summer of box office bombs. Who is green lighting this garbage? The scripts are terrible.

3:25 PM - 23 Jul 2013

★ LIKE A DOG ★

A JOURNEY INTO THE PRESIDENT'S FAVORITE SIMILE

Donald J. Trump
@realDonaldTrump
Following

.@DavidGregory got thrown off of TV by NBC, fired like a dog! Now he is on @CNN being nasty to me. Not nice!

11:10 PM - 29 Mar 2016

Donald J. Trump
@realDonaldTrump
Following

Egypt is a total mess. We should have backed Mubarak instead of dropping him like a dog.

2:48 PM - 12 Dec 2012

Donald J. Trump
@realDonaldTrump
Following

.@GlennBeck got fired like a dog by #Fox. The Blaze is failing and he wanted to have me on his show. I said no - because he is irrelevant.

11:09 PM - 16 Dec 2015

Donald J. Trump
@realDonaldTrump
Following

Robert Pattinson should not take back Kristen Stewart. She cheated on him like a dog & will do it again-- just watch. He can do much better!

2:47 PM - 17 Oct 2012

Donald J. Trump
@realDonaldTrump
Following

Mitt Romney had his chance to beat a failed president but he choked like a dog. Now he calls me racist-but I am least racist person there is

7:18 AM - 11 Jun 2016

Donald J. Trump
@realDonaldTrump
Following

Michael Wolff is a total loser who made up stories in order to sell this really boring and untruthful book. He used Sloppy Steve Bannon, who cried when he got fired and begged for his job. Now Sloppy Steve has been dumped like a dog by almost everyone. Too bad!

11:32 PM - 5 Jan 2018

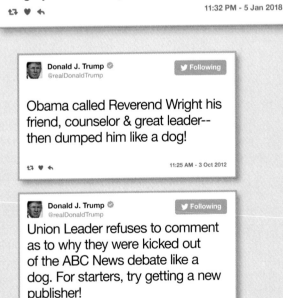

Donald J. Trump
@realDonaldTrump
Following

Obama called Reverend Wright his friend, counselor & great leader-- then dumped him like a dog!

11:25 AM - 3 Oct 2012

Donald J. Trump
@realDonaldTrump
Following

Union Leader refuses to comment as to why they were kicked out of the ABC News debate like a dog. For starters, try getting a new publisher!

6:23 PM - 10 Jan 2016

★ HOLIDAY CHEER ★

TIDINGS OF COMFORT AND JOY,
EVEN FOR THOSE WHO DON'T DESERVE IT

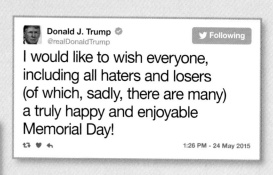

Donald J. Trump ✓
@realDonaldTrump
🐦 Following

I would like to wish everyone,
including all haters and losers
(of which, sadly, there are many)
a truly happy and enjoyable
Memorial Day!

1:26 PM - 24 May 2015

Donald J. Trump ✓
@realDonaldTrump
🐦 Following

I wish everyone, including the
haters and losers, a very happy
Easter!

2:24 AM - 5 Apr 2015

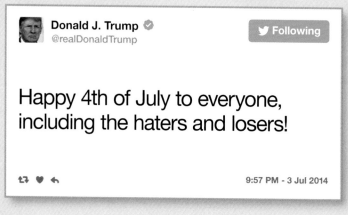

Donald J. Trump ✓
@realDonaldTrump
🐦 Following

Happy 4th of July to everyone,
including the haters and losers!

9:57 PM - 3 Jul 2014

Donald J. Trump ✓
@realDonaldTrump
🐦 Following

Happy Father's Day to all, even the
haters and losers!

4:43 PM - 15 Jun 2013

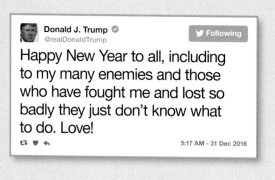

Donald J. Trump ✓
@realDonaldTrump
🐦 Following

Happy New Year to all, including
to my many enemies and those
who have fought me and lost so
badly they just don't know what
to do. Love!

5:17 AM - 31 Dec 2016

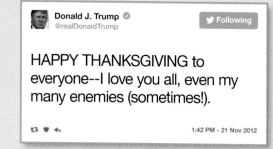

Donald J. Trump ✓
@realDonaldTrump
🐦 Following

HAPPY THANKSGIVING to
everyone--I love you all, even my
many enemies (sometimes!).

1:42 PM - 21 Nov 2012

WOW

★ **A GROWN MAN'S UNCANNILY CHILDLIKE SENSE OF WONDER** ★

Donald J. Trump @realDonaldTrump — Following

Wow—Family Feud said I am the third most envied man in America. I respectfully disagree—I am very modest.

2:08 PM - 15 Feb 2013

Donald J. Trump @realDonaldTrump — Following

Wow, Vanity Fair was totally shut out at the National Magazine Awards - it got NOTHING. Graydon Carter is a loser with bad food restaurants!

4:15 AM - 2 May 2014

Donald J. Trump @realDonaldTrump — Following

Wow! Does Eliot Spitzer have a girlfriend? This is getting exciting.

2:16 PM - 1 Aug 2013

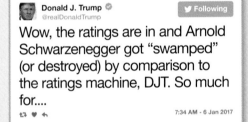

Donald J. Trump @realDonaldTrump — Following

Wow, the ratings are in and Arnold Schwarzenegger got "swamped" (or destroyed) by comparison to the ratings machine, DJT. So much for....

7:34 AM - 6 Jan 2017

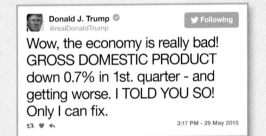

Donald J. Trump @realDonaldTrump — Following

Wow, the economy is really bad! GROSS DOMESTIC PRODUCT down 0.7% in 1st. quarter - and getting worse. I TOLD YOU SO! Only I can fix.

3:17 PM - 29 May 2015

Donald J. Trump @realDonaldTrump — Following

Wow, so many Fake News stories today. No matter what I do or say, they will not write or speak truth. The Fake News Media is out of control

4:29 AM - 4 Oct 2017

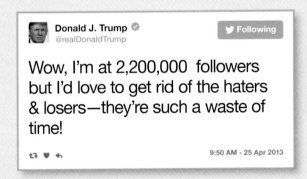

Donald J. Trump @realDonaldTrump — Following

Wow, I'm at 2,200,000 followers but I'd love to get rid of the haters & losers—they're such a waste of time!

9:50 AM - 25 Apr 2013

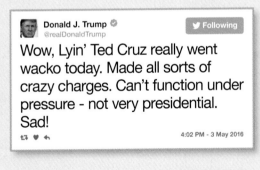

Donald J. Trump @realDonaldTrump — Following

Wow, Lyin' Ted Cruz really went wacko today. Made all sorts of crazy charges. Can't function under pressure - not very presidential. Sad!

4:02 PM - 3 May 2016

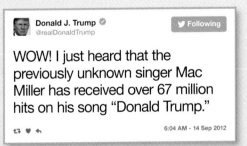

Donald J. Trump @realDonaldTrump — Following

WOW! I just heard that the previously unknown singer Mac Miller has received over 67 million hits on his song "Donald Trump."

6:04 AM - 14 Sep 2012

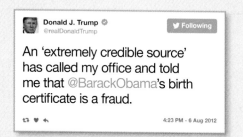

Donald J. Trump ✓
@realDonaldTrump
✔ Following

An 'extremely credible source' has called my office and told me that @BarackObama's birth certificate is a fraud.

4:23 PM - 6 Aug 2012

Donald J. Trump ✓
@realDonaldTrump
✔ Following

Let's take a closer look at that birth certificate. @BarackObama was described in 2003 as being "born in Kenya."

3:31 PM - 18 May 2012

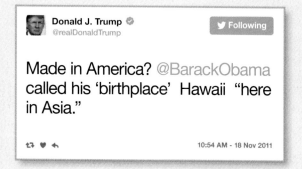

Donald J. Trump ✓
@realDonaldTrump
✔ Following

Made in America? @BarackObama called his 'birthplace' Hawaii "here in Asia."

10:54 AM - 18 Nov 2011

Donald J. Trump ✓
@realDonaldTrump
✔ Following

Why do the Republicans keep apologizing on the so called "birther" issue? No more apologies--take the offensive!

11:58 AM - 27 Aug 2012

Donald J. Trump ✓
@realDonaldTrump
✔ Following

I want to see @BarackObama's college records to see how he listed his place of birth in the application.

12:44 AM - 30 May 2012

Donald J. Trump ✓
@realDonaldTrump
✔ Following

What a coincidence--Michelle Obama called Kenya @BarackObama's "homeland" in 2008

10:02 AM - 29 Aug 2012

Donald J. Trump ✓
@realDonaldTrump
✔ Following

How amazing, the State Health Director who verified copies of Obama's "birth certificate" died in plane crash today. All others lived

4:32 PM - 12 Dec 2013

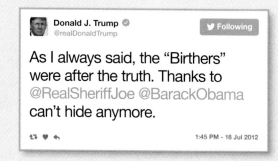

Donald J. Trump ✓
@realDonaldTrump
✔ Following

As I always said, the "Birthers" were after the truth. Thanks to @RealSheriffJoe @BarackObama can't hide anymore.

1:45 PM - 18 Jul 2012

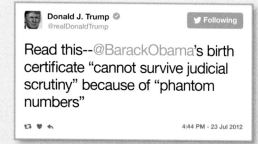

Donald J. Trump ✓
@realDonaldTrump
✔ Following

Read this--@BarackObama's birth certificate "cannot survive judicial scrutiny" because of "phantom numbers"

4:44 PM - 23 Jul 2012

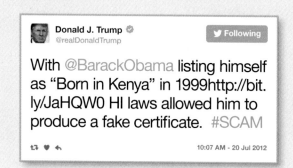

Donald J. Trump ✓
@realDonaldTrump
✔ Following

With @BarackObama listing himself as "Born in Kenya" in 1999http://bit.ly/JaHQW0 HI laws allowed him to produce a fake certificate. #SCAM

10:07 AM - 20 Jul 2012

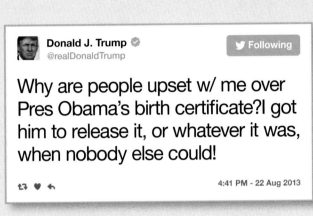

Donald J. Trump ✔
@realDonaldTrump
Following

Why are people upset w/ me over Pres Obama's birth certificate?I got him to release it, or whatever it was, when nobody else could!

4:41 PM - 22 Aug 2013

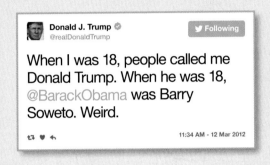

Donald J. Trump ✔
@realDonaldTrump
Following

When I was 18, people called me Donald Trump. When he was 18, @BarackObama was Barry Soweto. Weird.

11:34 AM - 12 Mar 2012

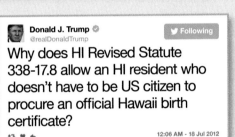

Donald J. Trump ✔
@realDonaldTrump
Following

Why does HI Revised Statute 338-17.8 allow an HI resident who doesn't have to be US citizen to procure an official Hawaii birth certificate?

12:06 AM - 18 Jul 2012

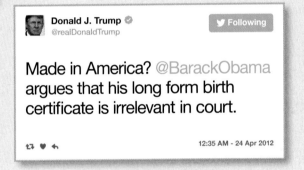

Donald J. Trump ✔
@realDonaldTrump
Following

Made in America? @BarackObama argues that his long form birth certificate is irrelevant in court.

12:35 AM - 24 Apr 2012

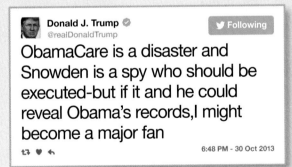

Donald J. Trump ✔
@realDonaldTrump
Following

ObamaCare is a disaster and Snowden is a spy who should be executed-but if it and he could reveal Obama's records,I might become a major fan

6:48 PM - 30 Oct 2013

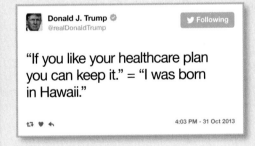

Donald J. Trump ✔
@realDonaldTrump
Following

"If you like your healthcare plan you can keep it." = "I was born in Hawaii."

4:03 PM - 31 Oct 2013

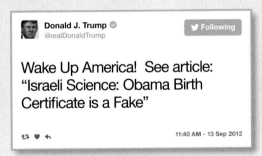

Donald J. Trump ✔
@realDonaldTrump
Following

Wake Up America! See article: "Israeli Science: Obama Birth Certificate is a Fake"

11:40 AM - 13 Sep 2012

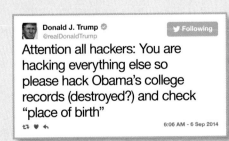

Donald J. Trump ✔
@realDonaldTrump
Following

Attention all hackers: You are hacking everything else so please hack Obama's college records (destroyed?) and check "place of birth"

6:06 AM - 6 Sep 2014

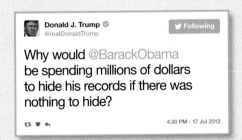

Donald J. Trump ✔
@realDonaldTrump
Following

Why would @BarackObama be spending millions of dollars to hide his records if there was nothing to hide?

4:30 PM - 17 Jul 2012

Donald J. Trump ✔
@realDonaldTrump
Following

Why won't Obama release his college applications? Is there something 'foreign' about them?

3:08 PM - 11 Sep 2012

★ ENIGMAS OF MAGA ★

TWEETS THAT MAKE YOU GO "HMMMM"

Donald J. Trump ✔
@realDonaldTrump
🐦 Following

Good.morning, I'm going to work!

5:59 AM - 13 Aug 2013

Donald J. Trump ✔
@realDonaldTrump
🐦 Following

The young intern who accidentally did a Retweet apologizes.

2:59 PM - 22 Oct 2015

Donald J. Trump ✔
@realDonaldTrump
🐦 Following

Why is this reporter touching me as I leave news conference? What is in her hand??

3:35 PM - 29 Mar 2016

Donald J. Trump ✔
@realDonaldTrump
🐦 Following

Something very important, and indeed society changing, may come out of the Ebola epidemic that will be a very good thing: NO SHAKING HANDS!

1:14 PM - 4 Oct 2014

Donald J. Trump ✔
@realDonaldTrump
🐦 Following

Sorry folks, I'm just not a fan of sharks - and don't worry, they will be around long after we are gone.

10:26 AM - 4 Jul 2013

Donald J. Trump ✔
@realDonaldTrump
🐦 Following

I don't like seeing the Pope standing at the checkout counter (front desk) of a hotel in order to pay his bill. It's not Pope-like!

11:46 AM - 19 Mar 2013

Donald J. Trump ✔
@realDonaldTrump
🐦 Following

We know who did the hoax of James Gandolfini and ObamaCare. Be careful, Mister.

1:16 PM - 20 Jun 2013

Donald J. Trump ✔
@realDonaldTrump
🐦 Following

I like Michael Douglas!

8:53 PM - 17 May 2016

TRUMPSTRADAMUS

Gaze into the crystal ball as Donald Trump tweets his predictions of the future! Was he right or was he wrong? HINT: He was right.

Donald J. Trump ✔
@realDonaldTrump
🐦 Following

Mexico will pay for the wall!

6:31 AM - 1 Sep 2016

RIGHT!

There is no wall, so technically, Mexico has covered all costs to date.

Donald J. Trump ✔
@realDonaldTrump
🐦 Following

Love making correct predictions. National Review is over.
http://theweek.com/articles/451963/national-…
review-doomed

8:39 PM - 23 Jan 2016

RIGHT!

This quote about the very much still-in-publication *National Review* is out of context. The president was of course saying, "The National Review is over . . . there on the newsstand." If Twitter had given him the extra characters he needed, you wouldn't have made that mistake.

Donald J. Trump ✔
@realDonaldTrump
🐦 Following

Everyone should calm down. @BenAffleck is going to do a great job as Batman.

2:43 PM - 18 Sep 2013

RIGHT!

Affleck's Batman did a great job introducing Wonder Woman, whom everyone loves.

Donald J. Trump ✔
@realDonaldTrump
🐦 Following

I predicted Apple's stock fall based on their dumb refusal to give the option of a larger iPhone screen like Samsung. I sold my Apple stock

6:49 AM - 28 Jan 2014

RIGHT!

This was a bold financial decision. By selling his Apple stock in early 2014, just before it more than doubled in value, Donald Trump

Donald J. Trump ✔
@realDonaldTrump
🐦 Following

Eventually, but at a later date so we can get started early, Mexico will be paying, in some form, for the badly needed border wall.

11:44 AM - 23 Apr 2017

ENOUGH ALREADY.

Of course Mexico will pay for the wall. The

THE JUMP TO 280
DOUBLING THE TREMENDOUSNESS

On November 7, 2017, a year after Trump's presidential victory, which many very bright people say was one of the biggest ever, Twitter made the medium-redefining decision to double its per-tweet character limit from 140 to 280. Among Trump Twitter cognoscenti, the move was as historic as it was divisive.

At right are two Trump tweets on the same topic, and two diverging arguments as to which is the superior. Remember, the debate on "140 v. 280" is like a Trump White House press conference: There are no "right answers" here.

THE "SHORT" ERA

Here we see how Twitter's original limits actually enhanced Trump's creativity—particularly when he focused on a deserving target (in this case, NPR leftist and former chest-hair exhibitionist Alec Baldwin). The tighter tweet's concision says to Baldwin: "Your existence merits neither my full attention nor my terrific energy." And yet in just 23 remaining characters, Trump still packs in a corrosive three-word democracy-delegitimizing conspiracy theory. If, as the very overrated William Shakespeare said, "Brevity is the soul of wit," then at 140 characters, Trump's soul thrives.

THE "LONG" ERA

No contest—only the 280-era Baldwin dispatch truly shows the time, effort, and thought that a sitting U.S. president devoted to harassing a mid-career actor. Where in the shorter format Baldwin merely "stinks," the more capacious parameters allow for compelling detailed descriptions of how Trump views his adversary: "dying," "mediocre," "terrible," worse than "Darrell Hammond." And while some feared that longer tweeting might seduce Trump into greater clarity, tweets like this put such concerns to rest. "Agony for those who were forced to watch"? Who conceivably was "forced" to watch *Saturday Night Live*? Even with 37 characters to spare, Trump leaves the answer alluringly unknown.

"PHONE TAPP"

4 MARCH 2017 – 7:02 AM

MEDIUM: TWITTER FOR ANDROID

DIMENSIONS: 135 CHARACTERS

"Phone Tapp" introduces itself to the observer with its titular "error," the typographic jazz of "tapp." But just as introductions blossom into deeper conversations, Trump's true intent soon unfolds like an orchid blossoming from swamp water. Trump frames the sacred and the bad (or sick) as twin ends of the lever, resting upon the playfully self-aware fulcrum of "Nixon/Watergate." Built upon such a chaotic frame, is the minor typographic defect bad? Sick? Or does the sick, conversely, become sacred?

"DUE PROCESS"

10 FEB 2018 – 10:33 AM

MEDIUM: TWITTER FOR IPHONE

DIMENSIONS: 264 CHARACTERS

Rendered amidst a worldwide movement based on believing women, "Due Process" bravely asks: "What if they're liars?" Infused with a lyrical, neo-Seussian rhythm, the work is a master class in contrast: True versus false. Old versus new. Due Process versus Trump's spectral desire to jail Hillary and the Central Park Five. Then, in a summary flourish, Trump ends on a question he has already answered. It's a tender eulogy to the countless fallen, like former White House Staff Secretary Rob Porter, whose life was destroyed simply because two ex-wives and an ex-girlfriend accused him of domestic violence, with merely one of them providing photographic evidence.

"WITCH HUNT"

27 FEB 2018 – 7:49 AM

MEDIUM: TWITTER FOR ANDROID

DIMENSIONS: 11 CHARACTERS

Composed just weeks after Twitter raised its limit from 140 to 280 characters, "Witch Hunt" rejected the new format in a terse, forceful 11—both a milestone formal achievement and an act of radical empathy. It is among Trump's greatest statements.

Here we see Trump's deep identification with, and compassion for, the oppression that women have suffered throughout history—for he, too, is being rashly victimized. With a mere two words, Trump rewrites Robert Mueller's failing hoax investigation as the contemptible descendant of Colonial America's greatest historical shame, when scores of seventeenth-century women were murdered for practicing witchcraft, despite there being only one real witch at that time: Hillary Clinton. (Look her up.)

The "Witch Hunt" theme is one to which the president would almost compulsively return (cf. March 19's "Total WITCH HUNT," April 10's "TOTAL WITCH HUNT!!!," April 22's "Complete Witch Hunt!," May 23's "WITCH HUNT!," etc.)—as though Trump felt that actually, he was possessed, and exorcism could be had only through relentless tweeting.

"BLEEDING BADLY"

29 JUNE 2017 – 8:52 AM, 8:58 AM

MEDIUM: TWITTER FOR IPHONE

DIMENSIONS: 140 CHARACTERS, 137 CHARACTERS

After six months of relative post-inauguration restraint, one can feel the pent-up energy in this mid-2017 pairing, in which Trump returns to his central themes: media bias (rampant), victimhood (his own), and, most important, female appearance (disgusting). Starting with a bracing shot of paradoxical surrealism (insisting he does not watch the TV show that he is live-tweeting), Trump then transports his audience to New Year's Eve at Mar-a-Lago—an elite institution now democratized for the reader, but never for the thrice-rejected Psycho Joe and Crazy Mika. The latter, of course, is the work's true subject: a figure to be both pitied and feared, her fictitiously "bleeding" face embodying both dishonest media artifice and Trump's lifelong phobia of menstruation and women generally.

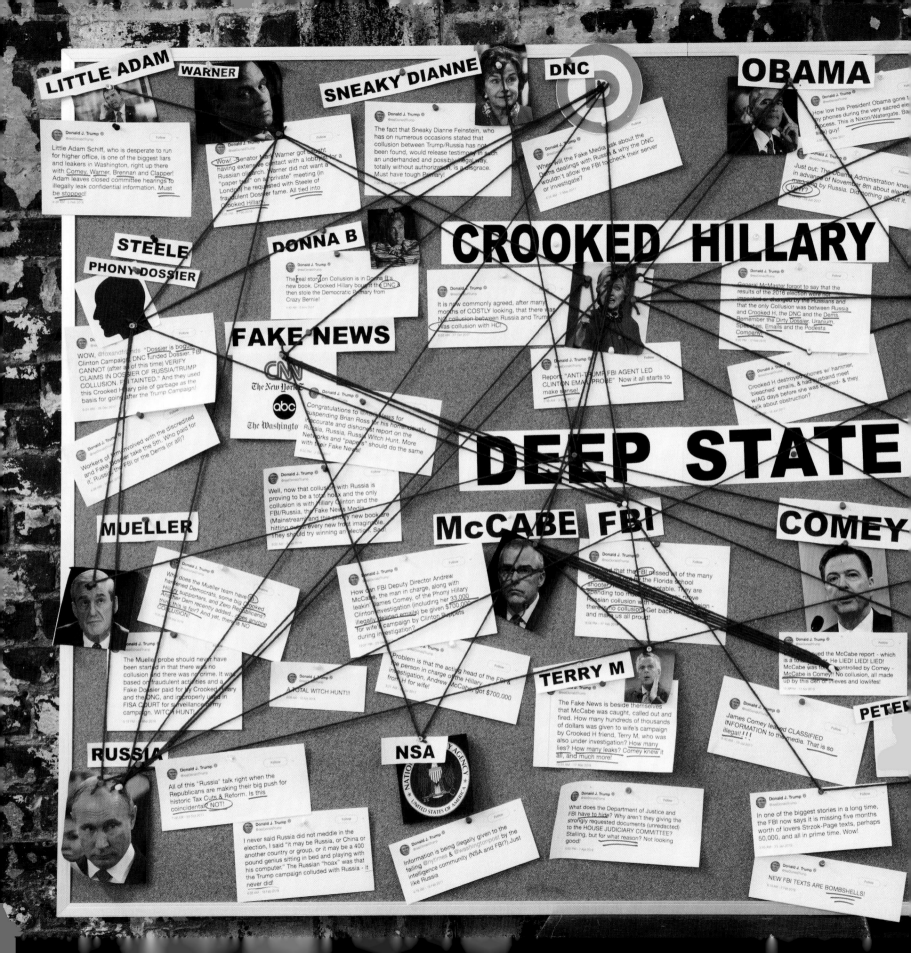

WAR AND TWEETS
THE *REAL* RUSSIA INVESTIGATION

From the moment Trump scored his huge electoral victory, which many are saying was the biggest they've ever seen, the so-called Russia "investigation" became the mainstream media's obsession. Its incessant "reporting" pushed Fake News "facts" like "Trump campaign officials pleading guilty" and "dead-to-rights collusion emails" from Trump's alleged "son." So the task of uncovering the truth fell to the president.

The real 2016 election scandal was the Deep State posing as the entire U.S. intelligence community in a devious and desperate effort to frame Trump for colluding with Russia—when there was No Collusion, which isn't even a crime, and the one who committed it was Hillary.

The trail of corruption was so clear. It led straight from James Comey through Loretta Lynch and Bill Clinton, plus DOJ's Sally Yates and FBI's Peter Strzok, on past an acronymia of intel agencies, then circling back to the Democratic Party, John Podesta, his brother, and from there pretty much directly, with a few other details, basically straight to Christopher "phony dossier" Steele. Then, to even more super-illegally prevent Trump from winning, add Spying on his Campaign by Obama's FBI, which for extra deviousness neither released nor acted on its Spy findings until after Trump had won.

The final puzzle piece would prove to be Robert Mueller, a hardened Democrat so anti-Trump that, just to seem impartial, he had been a registered Republican for fifty years.

★ ★ ★

COURTER'S LAST STAND

For more than two centuries, the American judicial system stood as the bedrock of democracy. But it would be no match for the Twitter onslaught of Donald Trump. With his brutally effective deployment of unconventional punctuation and "scare quotes," Trump proved he could easily vanquish "so-called judges" on the field of Twitter, even if the judges happened to sometimes win in so-called "courtrooms."

★ ★ ★

GLOBAL WARRING

Men can battle men, but only those who aspire to immortality, like Donald Trump, have the courage to take on the sky and air. In his war against the concept of climate change, Trump showed that massive barrages of peer-reviewed scientific research are no match for skillfully targeted tweets about occasional cold winter days.

★ ★ ★

THE BATTLE OF K-PATZ

As a Twitter superpower, Donald Trump sometimes found himself forced to take sides in conflicts he seemingly had nothing to do with. Trump's greatest intervention was in the 2012 battle between actor Robert Pattinson and his *Twilight* co-star Kristen Stewart. When Pattinson made the risky decision to forgive Stewart for cheating on him, the future President of the United States knew he had no choice but to take up arms, even where a less-confident leader might have considered the personal lives of two twentysomething screen actors none of his business.

★ ★ ★

THE PROBLEM WITH THOSE PEOPLE

Historically, the fields of professional American sports were tended by true patriots: Ruth, Mantle, Stockton, Havlicek, all the hockey guys . . . the list goes on. But in recent years a shadow fell over sports, as a small but vocal (not to say "mouthy") minority of belligerent, overpaid athletes tried to bring the nation to its knees. Yet these ungrateful sportsters were no match for America's Twitter Quarterback, number 45, Donald Trump. No longer would this particular group of degenerate jocks leave their black mark on America.

VERIFIED SURVIVORS

The president lied. Shocking but true. He called me far more often, and never once did I call him and he didn't return my call or get back to me in some manner. The more fun part though was that he said I wasn't smart. I probably spent a good thirty minutes hashing through and typing and then erasing and trying to come up with something witty and smart and cute that made the point that this was ridiculous and also that you're a fool. And so after multiple iterations of how I would respond to the president's tweet, I decided to go with "LOL."

—MARK CUBAN

Donald J. Trump @realDonaldTrump · Following

I know Mark Cuban well. He backed me big-time but I wasn't interested in taking all of his calls. He's not smart enough to run for president!

8:23 AM - 12 Feb 2017

On the morning that President Trump decided to tweet at me, I was in bible study and I got a call from my chief of staff, who read me the tweet. It was nothing more than a sexist smear intended to silence me. It was intended to silence over a dozen women who have credible assault and harassment allegations against Donald Trump, and the millions of women who have been protesting and marching ever since he became president. I went back to bible study and my colleagues said, "What was that about?" I said, "Well, the president just tweeted at me and basically called me a prostitute." Sadly, I'm in company with so many other women, but at the end of the day, the president will not silence any of us.

—SEN. KIRSTEN GILLIBRAND

Donald J. Trump @realDonaldTrump · Following

Lightweight Senator Kirsten Gillibrand, a total flunky for Chuck Schumer and someone who would come to my office "begging" for campaign contributions not so long ago (and would do anything for them), is now in the ring fighting against Trump. Very disloyal to Bill & Crooked-USED!

8:03 AM - 12 Dec 2017

Donald J. Trump @realDonaldTrump · Following

@Toure If you weren't such a dumb racist moron with bad ratings you would know I never filed for bankruptcy,now worth over $10 billion dummy

9:44 PM - 9 Sep 2013

Donald J. Trump @realDonaldTrump · Following

@Toure Dumb as a rock Toure doesn't have a clue about money or anything else-merely a simpleton racist. Really bad ratings,really stupid guy

9:53 PM - 9 Sep 2013

Donald J. Trump @realDonaldTrump · Following

@Toure Why does a network allow a stupid racist like Toure to stay on the air when his ratings are so abysmal! Can there be only one reason

10:10 PM - 9 Sep 2013

My social media bad habit was trolling Donald Trump on Twitter. I tweeted at him about declaring bankruptcy four times. A few hours later he tweeted, "Why does a network allow a stupid racist like Toure . . ." (see above). I don't know what that reason is, but okay. I wrote: "Is it weird that you can have so much money but still can't afford dignity?" After that day, Trump blocked me.

—TOURÉ

I don't really have a clear memory of when he attacked me with this tweet in 2012, because at the time he was just a grumpy misogynist and cable news addict who woke up early to spew his hate on Twitter. Now, not much has changed, except that grumpy misogynist spewing hate on Twitter is president. Despite all of his despicable actions, I would never say this country is going to hell. As for Trump himself, well, you'll have to be the judge of that.

—REP. DEBBIE WASSERMAN SCHULTZ

Donald J. Trump ✔
@realDonaldTrump   🐦 Following

Debbie Wasserman Schultz is hard to watch or listen to--no wonder our country is going to hell!

8:49 AM - 24 Feb 2012

Well, it happened. I'm Stephen King and Trump blocked me. I can no longer receive his thoughtful and incisive messages of love and inclusiveness. In short, I am an existential loser, waiting for Trump instead of Godot. I am, ladies and gentlemen, a Trump-less American.

—STEPHEN KING

Donald J. Trump ✔
@realDonaldTrump   🐦 Following

https://www.washingtonpost.com/news/arts-and-entertainment/wp/2017/06/13/trump-blocked-stephen-king-on-twitter-but-j-k-rowling-came-to-the-rescue/?utm_term=.29046f1c4357

8:23 AM - 12 Feb 2017

I used to think that his tweet about my nipples was one of the weirdest things I'd ever seen, but that pales on the weirdness scale compared to any week of the Trump administration. I was disappointed that he was, in effect, making fun of my weight, which I agree, had gone up, because I am a nervous eater and get fatter under stress. I would have thought that he understood that, because it is clear today, as he gets bigger and bigger because of the stress of his presidency, that he would be sympathetic to that. In fact, it seems to be legitimate to talk about his weight, not just because he's commented so freely on others, but because I am convinced it is an indicator of just how unhappy he is.

—FORMER REP. BARNEY FRANK

Donald J. Trump ✔
@realDonaldTrump   🐦 Following

Barney Frank looked disgusting--nipples protruding--in his blue shirt before Congress. Very very disrespectful.

3:35 PM - 21 Dec 2011

No, Donald Trump, this is not racism at its highest level. Slavery is racism at its highest level. The Holocaust is racism at its highest level. This is just the name of a television show. And that show, *Whiteish*, is called *Friends*—you know that show has already been made.

—KENYA BARRIS

Donald J. Trump ✔
@realDonaldTrump   🐦 Following

How is ABC Television allowed to have a show entitled "Blackish"? Can you imagine the furor of a show, "Whiteish"! Racism at highest level?

8:41 AM - 1 Oct 2014

When I reflect on this moment, my biggest regret is that he didn't give me a fun nickname. His tweet was just "Kathy Griffin." No "Unfunny Kathy" or "Ginger Kathy" or "Disgusting Kathy" or "Kooky Kathy." Just . . . Kathy. I'm sorry, I just really wanted an extra adjective, you know?
—**KATHY GRIFFIN**

> **Donald J. Trump** ✓
> @realDonaldTrump   🐦 Following
>
> Kathy Griffin should be ashamed of herself. My children, especially my 11 year old son, Barron, are having a hard time with this. Sick!
>
> 7:14 AM - 31 May 2017

Donald, every time I read your tweets and hear you on the TV, I struggle not to say the F word. I apologized once. I fucking regret it. You will be hearing from me every day until you leave office, so you better get used to it.
—**FMR. MEXICAN PRES. VICENTE FOX**

> **Donald J. Trump** ✓
> @realDonaldTrump   🐦 Following
>
> FMR PRES of Mexico, Vicente Fox horribly used the F word when discussing the wall. He must apologize! If I did that there would be a uproar!
>
> 3:27 PM - 25 Feb 2016

> **Donald J. Trump** ✓
> @realDonaldTrump   🐦 Following
>
> Former President Vicente Fox, who is railing against my visit to Mexico today, also invited me when he apologized for using the "f bomb."
>
> 9:07 AM - 31 Aug 2016

MELANIA TRUMP: TRYING TO HELP

The First Lady plays an important role in any presidency, and this was certainly true in the Trump Twitter Administration. Melania Trump took on a quintessentially twenty-first-century crusade: to end cyberbullying.

The phenomenon is well-known. Friendless losers with pitiable domination fantasies hide behind the safety of the screen to pick fights with people they would never have the courage to take on in real life, using personal attacks, threats of physical violence, and really dumb nicknames in a vain attempt to soothe their own insatiable insecurities. Sad.

The following is just a sampling of the pandemic vulgarity that Mrs. Trump worked so hard to combat.

@michellemalkin You were born stupid!

10:10 AM - 22 Mar 2013

I can't resist hitting lightweight @DannyZuker verbally when he starts up because he is just.so pathetic and easy (stupid)!

3:54 PM - 12 Jun 2013

Crazy Joe Biden is trying to act like a tough guy. Actually, he is weak, both mentally and physically, and yet he threatens me, for the second time, with physical assault. He doesn't know me, but he would go down fast and hard, crying all the way. Don't threaten people Joe!

6:19 AM - 22 Mar 2018

Finally, Liddle' Adam Schiff, the leakin' monster of no control, is now blaming the Obama Administration for Russian meddling in the 2016 Election. He is finally right about something. Obama was President, knew of the threat, and did nothing. Thank you Adam!

7:22 AM - 18 Feb 2018

Does anybody like Lyin' Ted?
https://www.instagram.com/p/BDqwFr_GhZJ/

2:45 PM - 1 Apr 2016

Some day, when things calm down, I'll tell the real story of @JoeNBC and his very insecure long-time girlfriend, @morningmika. Two clowns!

7:29 AM - 22 Aug 2016

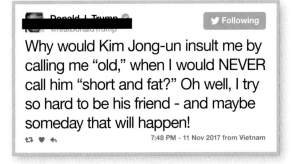
Why would Kim Jong-un insult me by calling me "old," when I would NEVER call him "short and fat?" Oh well, I try so hard to be his friend - and maybe someday that will happen!

7:48 PM - 11 Nov 2017 from Vietnam

I feel sorry for Rosie 's new partner in love whose parents are devastated at the thought of their daughter being with @Rosie--a true loser.

11:45 AM - 14 Dec 2011

@mcuban is very short off the tee - and his basketball sucks also!

7:15 AM - 19 Mar 2013

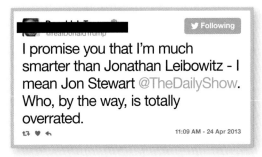
I promise you that I'm much smarter than Jonathan Leibowitz - I mean Jon Stewart @TheDailyShow. Who, by the way, is totally overrated.

11:09 AM - 24 Apr 2013

NOTE: *We have redacted the above perpetrators' identities, in the hope that they will change their ways in the future and not be forever linked to these regrettable tweets.*

"ILLEGAL VOTERS"

27 NOV 2016 – 3:30 PM

MEDIUM: TWITTER FOR ANDROID

DIMENSIONS: 140 CHARACTERS

What is reality? That—and nothing less—is the question so urgently posed by "Illegal Voters," the first undisputed masterpiece of Trump's controversial "President of the United States" period.

Here, concision masks a deceptively sophisticated structure. Trump first affirms conventional "facts" by citing his universally acknowledged electoral college victory. But already the trickster is tipping his hand: Note the sly subversion of "landslide" from its usual meaning to the exact opposite of that. This syntactic "error" quickly reveals itself as a rhetorical cliff's edge, off which Trump gleefully dives into an almost psychedelic fantasy world where he also won the popular vote, according to a hypothetical ("if you deduct the millions . . .") based on a known falsehood (about widespread voter fraud).

Tasting freedom as though for the first time, Trump builds his White House castle not just on sand, but imaginary sand. The viewer is left to ponder "Illegal Voters"' destabilizing effect on the world's oldest democracy, nurse a migraine, and perhaps answer emails from the very real Commission on Voter Fraud, whose multi-million-dollar, eight-month, results-less inquiry this tweet necessitated.

"BORN FUCKED UP"

28 SEP 2014 – 8:21 PM

MEDIUM: TWITTER FOR ANDROID

DIMENSIONS: 139 CHARACTERS

Arch, gratuitously profane, and clearly self-aware—okay, actually, this one's pretty funny. The man didn't become president for *no* reason. In 2014's "Born Fucked Up" we come across some of the Trumpiverse's most familiar characters—the "haters and losers"—to find that the Master of Fifth Avenue has compassionately reimagined what exactly their real problem is. A lesser man would attack such pathetic lowlife flecks of subhuman garbage, but Trump offers the scumbag degenerates only "love and affection," because that's how classy people handle jerks whose souls are bad.

"IMPEACH FOR GROSS INCOMPETENCE"

4 JUN 2014 - 6:23 AM

MEDIUM: TWITTER FOR ANDROID

DIMENSIONS: 62 CHARACTERS

Heralded as one of private citizen Trump's most provocative works, "Impeach for Gross Incompetence" found initial inspiration in President Barack Obama's 2014 deal to repatriate a captured American soldier. The tweet's elevation to Masterwork status, though, stems from how it has stood the test of time. What first appeared to be a tossed-off reaction to a minor news item has turned out to be a question for the ages, its doleful plea echoing ever stronger. "Are you allowed to impeach a president for gross incompetence?" Well, are you? ARE YOU? The world awaits the answer.

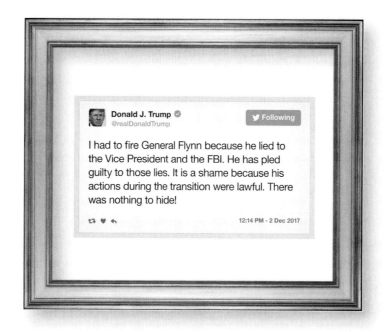

FORGERY ALERT "NOTHING TO HIDE"

2 DEC 2017 – 12:14 PM

MEDIUM: TWITTER FOR IPHONE

DIMENSIONS: 209 CHARACTERS

"Nothing To Hide" is a forgery, representing the only time, ever, that anyone other than the real Donald Trump has tweeted from the @realDonaldTrump account. We display it at the Trump Presidential Twitter Library as a reminder and a warning: Even the realest news can sometimes be fake.

Understanding this faux-Trump's origins is complicated, requiring deep knowledge of the phony Russia hoax that Democrats invented as an excuse for losing the election (which they did, big-time). The tale begins in February 2017, when President Trump says that he has fired General Flynn for lying to Vice President Pence about his (Flynn's) contacts with Russia. "I hope you can let this go," Trump reportedly tells FBI Director James Comey, who is investigating Flynn.

In this December 2017 tweet, however, Trump appears to say something different: that he fired Flynn not just for lying to the vice president—which is not a crime—but also for lying to the FBI—which is a crime. That would mean that Trump knew Flynn had broken the law when he told Comey to "let this go." And that could mean that "Nothing to Hide" would amount to Trump making an out-of-the-blue confession to obstruction of justice. Which would be truly insane.

Fortunately, Trump could not possibly have written the tweet, for one inarguable reason: His lawyer said he didn't.

Shortly after the Fake News obstruction argument emerged, Mr. Trump's personal attorney John Dowd stepped up to confess the truth. He had secretly taken over the account and written "Nothing to Hide" himself, in a passionate fit of forgetting every lawyer thing he ever knew.

The lesson: When authenticating social media works, we must judge the facts, and not merely how convenient and credulity-straining it seems that a lawyer on the president's personal payroll would access that president's Twitter account and tweet out this one thing, but never anything else. Let's move on.

11 MINUTES

It was only 11 minutes, but that was all it took to shatter a nation. On November 2, 2017, at 6:49 P.M., ET, President Trump's Twitter account vanished.

The day had begun like any other. In our nation's capital, citizens walked briskly across the Mall, their collars pulled up against the cold autumn wind as they gazed into a pale blue sky. We assume it was pale and blue. We couldn't really figure out how to google what the weather was like that day. But the probable seasonally appropriate chill in the air mirrored a greater chill to come. As the news spread around the world, disbelief turned to confusion, then shock, then dinner. By the time @realDonaldTrump was reactivated at 7:00 P.M., a disoriented America had stumbled untethered to its president for the better part of a quarter-hour.

We will never know for sure who or what caused Trump's account to go dark. One theory holds that a departing Twitter employee shut it down on his last day at work, since multiple sources identified him and he confirmed the story himself. But others suggest that we must look deeper, to man's aeons-old impulse to seek comfort in the shadows of ignorance. In this interpretation, we all are guilty, both in a moral sense and under all applicable state and federal laws.

The lasting tragedy of the Great Deactivation is that we will never know the damage's true extent. What tweetable thoughts crossed Donald Trump's mind? What transformative ideas or hot, fresh insults might have changed the course of world affairs? That wisdom is lost forever, because the sad fact is, during those terrible 11 minutes, Trump could compose no tweets. None. #NoneEleven.

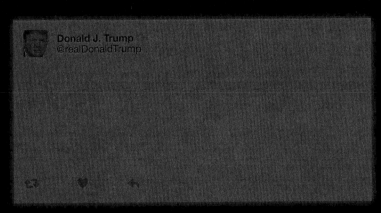

YOU TOO
CAN
BE A PART
OF
HISTORY

Long after publication of this volume, Donald Trump will keep making Twitter great again. Please paste the best of his later work into the beautiful frames on these pages.

Unlimited additional empty frames are available for free with purchase of more copies of this book.

TRUMP CROSSING THE DELAWARE

This iconic American masterpiece, painted in oil by Donald Trump himself, depicts his most loyal advisers following his detailed orders as they row across a river of liberal tears. As in life, Trump has surrounded himself with a diverse staff of loyal white people, each believing that he or she is the grownup keeping the boat from sinking.

Vice President Mike Pence and Chief of Staff John Kelly are shown frantically trying to dislodge ice while the president ignores Kelly and stomps squarely on Pence's testicles. At the bow sits Trump's daughter Ivanka, always nearby so the president can indulge in a long, non-creepy stare. Jeff Sessions, whom the president clearly regrets bringing, is tasked with helping son-in-law Jared Kushner keep the American Flag warm. The foreign policy team—Bolton, Mattis, Pompeo—huddle astern, envious that adviser Stephen Miller somehow gets to hold the rudder. Records are unclear as to how Kellyanne Conway stuck around through so many revisions to the painting, but she's still there and that's worth something. Sarah Huckabee Sanders, meanwhile, has never been happier.

Modern X-ray analysis has revealed that an earlier version of the work showed Vladimir Putin in the water, shirtless and single-handedly tugging the boat wherever he wants it to go, but this was later covered up.

ACKNOWLEDGMENTS

The editors would like to thank everyone at Spiegel & Grau for their enthusiasm, flexibility, and support, especially Evan Camfield, Annie Chagnot, Richard Elman, Matthew Martin, Greg Mollica, Simon Sullivan, and the amazing Julie Grau.

Big-league thanks also to Comedy Central for its help not only with getting this book done, but also with the physical Library itself. Specifically: Steve Albani, Emily Albertson, Kent Alterman, Joe Babbino, Sarah Babineau, Aileen Budow, Matt Conte, Jonah Delso, Nina Di Leo, Yvette Encarnacion, Kathy Fusco, Mike Gelsomino, Tanya Giles, Akash Goyal, Matt Herrlett, Deborah Lake, Eve Kenny, Josh Line, Renata Luczak, Wanda McSwain, Ari Pearce, Steve Raizes, Megan Ring, Lane Savage, Chris Scarlata, Chiara Seward, Shawn Silverman, Michael Stanger, Matt Silvestri, Cynthia Thomas, Andrea Torres, Julie Verardi, Adam Wactlar, and Amanda Wolfe. A special shout-out for the all-nighters pulled by designers Angelina Battista, Paulina Niewinska, Erin Smith, and the tireless Donna Tine.

The IRL exhibit was realized by Pop2Life with the extraordinary vision and talent of Jeff Bardin, Seth Bellaff, Anthony "Dob" Dobrini, Jen Gotti, and Alicia Haberman.

The entire Library project couldn't have happened without *The Daily Show with Trevor Noah*'s top-flight staff. We'd like to thank Kaitlin Alm, Stacey Angeles, Russ Armstrong, Nick Bailey, Ian Berger, Juan Boria, Eric Bowron, Chris Brown, Max Browning, Kristen Bunk, Vilma Cardenas, Kashana Cauley, Justin Chabot, Ronny Chieng, Mike Choi, Franco Coello, Amir Combs, Lisa Cortez, Eliza Cossio, LaToia Cunningham, Eric Davies, Pam DePace, Sebastian DiNatale, Jimmy Donn, Tom Dowling, Justine Elena, Maia Erickson, Tom Favilla, Christy Fiero, Graham Frazier, Sean Gallagher, GDBA, George Gountas, Jeff Gussow, Hallie Haglund, Sarah Hamblin, Lorenzo Hansford, Camille Hebert, Scott Hercman, Kira Klang Hopf, Sebastian Ischer, Nik Johnson, Jessie Kanevsky, Jill Katz, David Kibuuka, Jordan Klepper, Michael Kosta, Madeleine Kuhns, Christina Kyriazis, Devin Leary, Tim Lester, Susan Locke-Shapiro, John Lott, Angelo Lozada, Desi Lydic, Allison MacDonald, Christiana Mbakwe, Dennis McMahon, Justin Melkmann, David Paul Meyer, Ryan Middleton, Hasan Minhaj, Jody Morlock, Afeef Nessouli, Chuck O'Neil, RJ Osterhoudt, Mark Paone, Owen Parsons, Christina Pelletiere, Felipe Pena, Paul Pennolino, Ryan Phillips, Matt Polidoro, Lindsay Quella, Tim Quigley, Brittany Radocha, Paul Ranieri, Chris Rose, Phil Salanto, Mike Schmehl, Enid Seymore, Erin Shannon, Dulcé Sloan, Patty Smith, Craig Spinney, Brandon Stefanowitz, Sara Taksler, Glenn Tartaglia, Adriane Truex, Shannon Turgeon, Marilyn Vigilante, Misha Vool, Juliet Werner, Einar Westerlund, Mike Williams, Nate Witmer, Michelle Wolf, Roy Wood Jr., Fiona Wozniak, Rich York, and Rob York.

Thanks also to CAA (Andy Elkin, C. C. Hirsch, Cait Hoyt, David Larabell, Rachel Rusch), UTA (Greg Cavic), Schreck, Rose, Dapello & Adams LLC (Nancy Rose, Carolyn Conrad), and Norm Aladjem, Derek Van Pelt, Sanaz Yamin, and everyone at Mainstay Entertainment.

A special thanks to all our Verified Survivors for bravely recounting their experiences.

We especially h/t Twitter for existing and, on a smaller scale, accommodating our requests.

And of course we'd be utterly remiss, and possibly deported, if we failed to acknowledge the true genius contributions of President Donald J. Trump. ('Sup Dan Scavino yeah we know you're out there.)

Finally, a very special thanks to our tremendous host, Trevor Noah, who back in 2015 was the first at *TDS* to recognize that DJT was, in fact, going to become our Commander-In-Tweet.

PHOTO AND ART CREDITS

Cover · Frame by Iakov Filimonov/Shutterstock, Background by GraphicaArtis/Getty Images, Photos from left to right by Drew Angerer/Getty Images, Samuel Corum/Anadolu Agency via Getty Images, John Thys/AFP via Getty Images, Michael Brochstein/SOPA Images/LightRocket via Getty Images, Alex Wong/Getty Images, Win McNamee/Getty Images, Aaron P. Bernstein/Getty Images, Michael Reynolds-Pool/Getty Images, Timothy A. Clary/AFP via Getty Images, Drew Angerer/Getty Images, Alex Wong/Getty Images, Mark Wilson/Getty Images. Designed by Joe Dettmore, The Daily Show with Trevor Noah, Composited by Greg Mollica, S&G. **Page ii** · Sculpture by Justin Chabot, The Daily Show with Trevor Noah, photo by Rob Kim/Getty Images. **iv** · photo by Jeff Schear/Getty Images. **vi-vii** · Graphic Illustrations by Joe Dettmore, The Daily Show with Trevor Noah. **viii-ix** · Background by KazanovskyAndrey/iStock via Getty Images. **x** · Photo by Nick Dyer, Comedy Central. **xii** · Photo by Scott Olson/Getty Images. **xiv** · Graphic Illustration by Michelle Willems/Comedy Central. **1** · Photo by Bettmann/Getty Images. **2** · Photo by Amanda Schwab/StarPix/REX via Shutterstock. **3** · Photo by Chip Somodevilla/Getty Images. **4** · Photo by Rob Kim/Getty Images. **5** · Letter provided by Mike Tollin, Trump Photo by George Napolitano/FilmMagic via Getty Images. **6** · Obama's Birth Certificate via obamawhitehouse.archives.gov. **7** · Photo by Mark Makela/Getty Images. **8** · From left to right, Paul Faith/AFP via Getty Images, Saul Loeb/AFP via Getty Images. **9** · Photo by Drew Anger/Getty Images. **12-19** · Birth of a Birther Frame by Lane Savage/Comedy Central, 9/11 Haters and Losers Frame by Ekely/E+ via Getty Images, Taco Bowls Frame by Tomekbudujedomek/Moment via Getty Images, Lyin' Ted Frame by Tomekbudujedomek/Moment via Getty Images. **23-33** · Medals Designed by The Daily Show with Trevor Noah, Arranged by Pop2Life, Photos by Lane Savage/Comedy Central, Frames by leezsnow/E+ via Getty Images. **34-37** · Illustrations by Boris Rasin, Frames by ChrisAt/E+ via Getty Images, Backgrounds by Pinghung Chen/EyeEm via Getty Images. **36-39** · Background by GOLDsquirrel/iStock via Getty Images, Plaques by pzAxe/iStock via Getty Images. **40-45** · Exhibit photo by Sean Gallagher, The Daily Show with Trevor Noah, Map by gio_banfi/DigitalVision Vectors via Getty Images, Flags by pop_jop/DigitalVision Vectors via Getty Images. **51** · Created by Pop2Life/The Daily Show with Trevor Noah, Exhibit photo by Sean Gallagher, The Daily Show with Trevor Noah. **52–61** · Covfefe Frame by Lane Savage/Comedy Central, Nobody Has More Respect Frame by Ekely/E+ via Getty Images, Composition In Meme And Bodyslam Frame by Tomekbudujedomek/Moment via Getty Images, My Button Works Frame by Tomekbudujedomek/Moment via Getty Images, Very Stable Genius Frame by goir/iStock via Getty Images. **62–63** · Graphic Illustration by Dave Heiss/The Daily Show with Trevor Noah, Background Texture by Juhku/iStock via Getty Images. Page **64–65** · Pillar photo by ipopba/iStock via Getty Images Plus, Background by noppadon_sangpeam/iStock via Getty Images. **66–67** · Graphic Illustration by Katie Hall/The Daily Show with Trevor Noah, photos by sirapob/iStock via Getty Images, Xinzheng/Moment via Getty Images, sorendls/E+ via Getty Images, Xinzheng/Moment via Getty Images, Natalia Bazani/EyeEm via Getty Images, Wavebreakmedia/iStock via Getty Images, michaeljung/iStock via Getty Images. **70** · Left to right, photos by Michael Loccisano/Getty Images, Mark Wilson/Getty Images, Joe Kohen/Getty Images, Theo Wargo/Getty Images. **71** · Top to bottom, photos by Steffi Loos/Getty Images, Dimitrios Kambouris/Getty Images, Paul Morigi/Getty Images, Spencer Platt/Getty Images, Theo Wargo/Getty Images, Mario Tama/Getty Images, Monica Schipper/Getty Images, Mike Windle/Getty Images, Paul Morigi/Getty Images. **85** · Photo by Sean Gallagher/The Daily Show with Trevor Noah. **86** · Graphic Illustration by Katie Hall/The Daily Show with Trevor Noah, photos by Fine Art Images/Heritage Images via Getty Images, Nicholas Kamm/AFP via Getty Images. **89** · Frames by ChrisAt/E+ via Getty Images. **90–97** · Phone Tapp Frame by Lane Savage/Comedy Central, Due Process Frame by Ekely/E+ via Getty Images, Witch Hunt Graphic Illustration by Joe Dettmore/The Daily Show with Trevor Noah, Photos by Jewel Samad/AFP via Getty Images, Universal History Archive/UIG via Getty Images, The New York Historical Society via Getty Images, Bleeding Badly Frame by Tomekbudujedomek/Moment via Getty Images. **98–99** · Created by Ramin Hedayati and Matt Negrin/The Daily Show with Trevor Noah, Photo by Lane Savage/Comedy Central, Clockwise starting from top left, photos by Alex Wong/Getty Images, Win McNamee/Getty Images, Johnny Louis/WireImage via Getty Images, Mark Wilson/Getty Images, Alex Wong/Getty Images, Peter Macdiarmid/AFP via Getty Images, Melina Mara/The Washington Post via Getty Images, Dean Mouhtaropoulos/Getty Images, John Moore/Getty Images, Mark Wilson/Getty Images, Paul J. Richards/AFP via Getty Images, Brendan Smialowski/AFP via Getty Images, Chip Somodevilla/Getty Images, Jung Yeon-Je/AFP via Getty Images, Al Drago/CQ Roll Call via Getty Images, Nicholas Kamm/AFP via Getty Images, Katherine Frey/The Washington Post via Getty Images, Jim Watson/AFP via Getty Images, Paul J. Richards/AFP via Getty Images, Mikhail Svetlov/Getty Images, Saul Loeb/AFP via Getty Images, other elements provided by jakkapan21/iStock via Getty Images, kolae/iStock via Getty Images. **100–107** · Medals Designed by Michael Hogan/The Daily Show with Trevor Noah, Arranged by Pop2Life, Photos by Lane Savage/Comedy Central, Frames by leezsnow/E+ via Getty Images. **108–110** · Mark Cuban photo by Allen Berezovsky/Getty Images, Touré image courtesy of Touré, Official Headshot of Kirsten Gillibrand provided by her office, Official Headshot of Debbie Wasserman Schultz provided by her office, Stephen King photo by Leigh Vogel/WireImage via Getty Images, Barney Frank photo by Ray Tamarra/GC Images via Getty Images, Kenya Barris photo by Mike Coppola/Getty Images, Kathy Griffin photo by Paul Morigi/WireImage via Getty Images, Vicente Fox photo by Allen Berezovsky/Getty Images, frames by Beeldbewerking/iStock via Getty Images. **110–111** · All nametag photos by Sean Gallagher, The Daily Show with Trevor Noah. **112** · Photo by Chip Somodevilla/Getty Images. **114–119** · Illegal Voters Frame by Lane Savage/Comedy Central, Born Fucked Up Frame by Ekely/E+ via Getty Images, Impeach For Gross Incompetence Frame by Tomekbudujedomek/Moment via Getty Images. **120–121** · Frame by catnap72/E+ via Getty Images. **125** · Frames by JoKMedia/E+ via Getty Images. **126** · Frame by ISMODE/iStock via Getty Images. For photos, see "Cover." **129** · Photo by Rob Kim/Getty Images **130** · Created by Pop2Life/The Daily Show with Trevor Noah, photo by Anthony Dobrini/Pop2Life.

Copyright © 2018 by Comedy Partners
Foreword copyright © 2018 by Merewether LLC

All rights reserved.

Published in the United States by Spiegel & Grau, an imprint of Random House, a division of Penguin Random House LLC, New York.

SPIEGEL & GRAU and colophon is a registered trademark of Penguin Random House LLC.

Hardback ISBN 978-1-9848-0188-3
Ebook ISBN 978-1-9848-0189-0

Printed in the United States of America on acid-free paper

spiegelandgrau.com
randomhousebooks.com

9 8 7 6 5 4 3 2 1

First Edition

IN MEMORIAM

ALTHOUGH ALL TRUMP TWEETS ARE PERFECT, SOME WERE TOO PERFECT TO LAST.
HERE LIES A SELECTION OF TWEETS DELETED BEFORE THEIR TIME.